STOKES
Beginner's Guide
to Shorebirds

Donald and Lillian Stokes   *MAPS BY* **Thomas Young**

Little, Brown and Company
Boston   New York   London

First Edition

Library of Congress Cataloging-in-Publication Data
Stokes, Donald W.
    Stokes beginner's guide to shorebirds / by Donald and Lillian Stokes; maps by Thomas Young.—1st ed.
        p.   cm.
    ISBN 0-316-81696-5
    1. Shorebirds—North America—Identification.   I. Stokes, Lillian Q.   II. Title.
    QL681 .S73 2001
    598.3'3'097—dc21   00-053467

10 9 8 7 6 5 4 3 2 1

TWP

Printed in Singapore

Photo Credits

Here is a list of the photographers whose wonderful photographs bring the beauty and details of shorebirds up close. The letter or letters following a page number refer to the position of the picture on the page (T=top; B=bottom; L=left; C=center; R=right). A second number in parentheses after a credit indicates that the photo also appears as a silhouette in the Color Tab Index or Clues pages.

Herbert Clarke: 121TR, 47, 63BL, 103TR, 107TL.
Mike Danzenbaker: 37BR (1), 41B, 41TR, 43B, 51R, 53B, 53TR (35), 55BR, 61BR, 61TL (59), 61TR (59), 63BR, 67BL (58), 67BR, 67TR, 75B, 75TR, 81B, 81TL, 83R, 85TL (73), 85TR, 87B, 93BR, 93TR, 95 (73), 99R, 101BC, 103BR, 107B, 107TR, 109B, 109TR (97), 111BR, 111L (97), 111TR, 113BR, 117R, 123BR, 123TR (118), 125B, 129TL, 135BR, 135TL, 139BR, 142R, 143R.
Kevin Karlson: 37BL (1, 34), 39B, 45BR, 49R, 55TL, 55TR, 63TL, 63TR (59), 65BR, 65TL, 65TR, 71 (58), 77BR, 87TR (73), 93BL, 93TL, 101BR, 101TR, 115R, 117L (97), 123L, 127L (118), 129TR, 131BL, 133BL, 133BR, 133TL, 135TR (119), 137L, 139TL, 141TR.
Clair Postmus: 43TR, 51L (35), 65BL (1, 58), 77BL (1, 72), 77TL (72), 77TR, 87TL, 101BL (1, 96), 101TL (96), 121BR, 125TL (118), 125TR, 127R, 129BL (1, 119), 131TR (119), 139BL (1, 119).
Brian Small: 37TL, 41TL (34), 45L (35), 53TL, 55BL, 57B, 57TL, 57TR, 61BL, 69 (58), 75TL (72), 79L (72), 79R, 83BL, 89BL, 89R (73), 89TL, 91BL, 91BR, 105L, 105R, 113L (97), 113TR, 115L (97), 131BR, 135BL, 137R (119), 142L, 143L.
Lillian Stokes: 141BR.
Tom Vezo: 37TR, 39TL, 39R (34), 43TL (3, 34), 45TR, 49L (35), 67TL, 81TR (73), 83TL, 85B, 91TL, 91TR, 99L (96), 103L, 109TL, 121L (118), 129BL, 131TL, 133TR (119), 139TR, 141BL, 141TL (119).

Large Shorebirds 14–23"

(About the size of a crow.) These birds generally have long legs and long bills. Many are "unmistakables" because of distinctive bill shapes or colors, or leg colors.

Example: Willet

Medium Shorebirds 8½–12"

(About the size of a robin.) Look at bill length to place in subgroups.

Bill considerably longer than head

Example: Dowitcher

Bill about as long as head

Example: Red Knot

Example: Black-bellied Plover

Bill clearly shorter than head

Small Shorebirds 6–8"

(About the size of a sparrow.) Tiny, move fast, have short legs and short to medium bills.

Examples: Sanderling   **Least Sandpiper**

Stokes Field Guides

Stokes Field Guide to Birds: Eastern Region

Stokes Field Guide to Birds: Western Region

Stokes Field Guide to Bird Songs: Eastern Region (CD/cassette)

Stokes Field Guide to Bird Songs: Western Region (CD/cassette)

Stokes Beginner's Guides

Stokes Beginner's Guide to Bats

Stokes Beginner's Guide to Birds: Eastern Region

Stokes Beginner's Guide to Birds: Western Region

Stokes Beginner's Guide to Butterflies

Stokes Beginner's Guide to Dragonflies

Stokes Beginner's Guide to Shorebirds

Stokes Backyard Nature Books

Stokes Bird Feeder Book

Stokes Bird Gardening Book

Stokes Birdhouse Book

Stokes Bluebird Book

Stokes Butterfly Book

Stokes Hummingbird Book

Stokes Oriole Book

Stokes Purple Martin Book

Stokes Wildflower Book: East of the Rockies

Stokes Wildflower Book: From the Rockies West

Stokes Nature Guides

Stokes Guide to Amphibians and Reptiles

Stokes Guide to Animal Tracking and Behavior

Stokes Guide to Bird Behavior, Volume 1

Stokes Guide to Bird Behavior, Volume 2

Stokes Guide to Bird Behavior, Volume 3

Stokes Guide to Enjoying Wildflowers

Stokes Guide to Nature in Winter

Stokes Guide to Observing Insect Lives

Other Stokes Books

The Natural History of Wild Shrubs and Vines

Contents

How to Use This Guide

Stokes Beginner's Guide to Shorebirds is a handy guide to identifying the major species of shorebirds found in North America. This includes the 49 regularly seen species and 4 that are only rarely seen.

"Marker Birds"

Identifying shorebirds is easiest if you can get some idea of the size of the bird you are watching. In the Color Tab Index we have given you some measurements and comparisons with other common birds — crows, robins, sparrows — but these species are not usually near shorebirds. The best way to determine size in shorebirds is to learn to identify a few of the more common and easily recognizable species. These then become what we call "marker birds" — shorebirds that you use as a sort of measuring stick with which to compare the size of other shorebirds. Marker birds are indicated in the Clues at the beginning of each color tab section.

Some of the best marker birds in each size category are:

Large birds — Willet
Medium birds — Killdeer, Black-
    bellied Plover
Small birds — Sanderling, Least
    Sandpiper, Semipalmated Plover

In practically any group of shore-birds, there is one of these species. When looking over a group of shore-birds, look for marker birds first; this will make it easier to sort out the rest of the birds by size.

Color Tab Index and Clues Pages

Use the Color Tab Index to help you decide the size of the bird you are trying to identify and, in the case of medium-sized birds, the relative length of the bird's bill. Long bills are twice the depth of the head; medium bills are about the depth of the head; and short bills are clearly shorter than the depth of the head. (The depth of the head is the distance from the base of the bill to the back of the head.)

Then turn to the first two pages of the appropriate color tab section, where you will find the Clues pages. These are designed to help you either make the identification right away or narrow down your possible choices. Check your final identification by turning to the species accounts in that section.

Silhouettes

Inside the back cover is a silhouette guide to the main shorebirds included in this book. In a few cases, when the silhouettes of two or more birds are extremely similar, the birds are represented by a single silhouette (for example, American and Black Oystercatcher are both represented by the silhouette labeled Oystercatchers). These drawings are true to life since they are based on tracings of photographs. They have been arranged in order of their relative size, from largest to smallest, according to the length of the bird.

Species Descriptions

All of the major species have complete identification descriptions. The common name of the bird is followed by the scientific name and the bird's length. Length is a measurement of the bird from the tip of the tail to the tip of the bill.

Because most shorebirds undergo seasonal plumage variation, we have divided many of the detailed clues to their identification into seasonal sections. **Main Year-round Clues** describe features that apply to the adult bird regardless of season. **Additional Summer Clues** describe features that can further aid identification when the birds are in their breeding plumage (roughly March through August). **Additional Winter Clues** describe features that can further aid identification when the birds are in their nonbreeding plumage (roughly September through February).

Some species of shorebirds have distinctive juvenal plumages and these are mentioned under the heading **Juvenile**. (Juvenal plumage is the first full set of feathers of a young bird after it loses its natal down.)

Under the heading **In Flight** are clues to help you identify a bird on the wing. This is sometimes very helpful, since shorebirds do a lot of flying.

And **Call** is an approximation of the most common sounds made by that species.

Range and Migration Maps

The range and migration maps that accompany each species description are special innovations of this guide. We have included them because the majority of our shorebirds breed in the Arctic and winter in South America. Thus, our best time to see them is during migration. In addition, shorebirds are very easy to observe as they migrate — they are active during the day, they often gather in large flocks, and they often feed in open areas such as beaches or mudflats.

Key to the Maps

Most species accounts include two maps with these features:

- The yellow-shaded area shows the summer, or breeding, range.
- The blue-shaded area shows the winter, or nonbreeding, range. (Some birds may remain on their wintering grounds during their first summer.)
- The green area shows the year-round range, where a species breeds and spends the winter.
- The dotted lines and the dates beside them show where and when a species occurs during

Apr 1
Mar 15
Mar 1

Spring
Migration

migration. (See below for more detailed information on how to interpret these lines.)

- The spring migration map shows the routes and timing of a species as the bird flies north, the fall map shows the routes and timing of a species as it flies south.

Below each map there is also a sentence or two containing more information about the migration of the species; this information may be on any of several topics, such as:

- Habitat used during migration
- Duration of migration
- Size of the flocks in which the species is typically seen
- Whether the species is found in mixed flocks
- Differences in timing of migration between similar species
- Whether the species is often seen outside its migration path

Additional Information on the Red Dotted Lines

Migration route — The red dotted lines are drawn across the entire width of a species' regular migration route. If a map has long lines drawn from coast to coast, then this species can be seen all across the country. Short lines indicate a narrower migration route and a more limited area in which the bird can be commonly seen. For many species, fall and spring migration routes are different.

Shorebirds can wander widely during migration, so individuals and small flocks may be seen outside a species' regular migration route.

Timing of the first major wave of migrants — The date that appears by each red line tells when the first major wave of migrants of a species arrives in that area. These dates are averages based on many years of field observation by hundreds of observers. Individuals and small flocks may arrive earlier and other waves may occur later.

Generally, the dates are presented in half-month intervals, as this makes the map easily readable. In a few cases one-month intervals are shown because migration of that species is moving slowly at that time and there is no room to clearly put in the half-month interval.

Several weather-related factors may alter the timing of migration. For instance, a storm front may cause birds to delay their departure. Also, a warm front may trigger early northward movement, while a cold front may trigger early southward movement. Wind and rain are also factors. Tailwinds help migrating birds fly more quickly and arrive at their destination sooner,

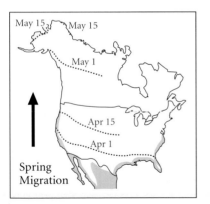

while headwinds may slow migration. Very strong winds, regardless of direction, can temporarily stop birds (especially smaller birds) from migrating. A steady rain can also bring migration to a temporary halt. Fog has the same effect.

Depending on which of these factors come into play, you may notice the first major wave of a species in your area arriving either before or after the dates shown on the maps.

Photographs and Silhouettes

Photographs have been carefully chosen to represent the most important plumages that the average observer is likely to see. Every shorebird species has a variety of plumages and conditions of plumage, and it would be impossible to include them all in any guide. And remember that each individual shorebird can look slightly different from others of its species; whether you are using a drawn picture or a photograph for identification, it is only a representation of one bird. In every case, we have tried to pick photographs that best represent a species.

Since many shorebirds are similar in plumage, obvious or even subtle differences in their shapes and proportions can be extremely helpful to identification. It is easiest to see these differences through silhouettes. Thus, each bird's identification page includes its silhouette. Occasionally, we have added silhouettes of other species for comparison when we thought it would be helpful.

What Is a Shorebird?

Shorebirds are a group of closely related species of birds that have tremendous variation in outward appearance. They are all in the order Charadriiformes, which also includes, among others, gulls, terns, puffins, murres, skimmers, and jaegers.

The shorebird species in this guide fall into four different families:

Charadriidae: plovers (9 species)
Haematopodidae: oystercatchers (2 species)
Recurvirostridae: avocet and stilt (2 species)
Scolopacidae: yellowlegs, Willet, tattler, sandpipers, Whimbrel, curlew, godwits, turnstones, Surfbird, knot, Sanderling, stints, Dunlin, dowitchers, snipe, woodcock, and phalaropes (40 species)

These birds are grouped together because of structural similarities in the characteristics of their skull, backbones, and syrinx (sound-making organ). Of course, none of these characteristics are apparent to the casual observer. And because shorebirds vary so much in size, shape, color, habitat, and behavior, it is hard to make a general definition of this group without also having to mention the many exceptions.

In spite of this, here is a list of traits that are shared by the majority of North American shorebirds:

- Cryptically colored with browns, grays, and whites
- Simple vocalizations such as peeps, whistles, or short trills
- Probe in mud with their bills or pick prey off the surface of the ground
- Thin pointed bills
- Live and feed near the water's edge
- Breed and winter in open areas
- Sexes look similar
- Nest in a scrape made in the ground
- Breed in the far north or Arctic
- Long-distance migrants
- Have pointed wings and are strong fliers
- Those with long bills often have long legs

- Can run short distances well
- Winter along lakes or ocean shorelines
- Often in large flocks during nonbreeding months.

In summary, trying to define what exactly is a shorebird is rather difficult. It is almost easier and truer to say, "You'll know one when you see one."

How to Identify Shorebirds

Shorebirds are such a beautiful group of birds. Their graceful forms, exquisite synchronized flight, haunting calls, and habitats of wide open spaces make them spectacular birds to be near and enjoy.

Being able to identify the various species adds greatly to the richness of the experience and can give you a handle for accumulating information and observations about their intriguing lives.

Most people have a hard time identifying shorebirds. Shorebirds can all seem to look alike, and when hundreds are grouped together it can feel a bit overwhelming as you try to sort them out. This is what we sometimes refer to as "shorebird anxiety." And it is understandable, since very few field guides really give the beginner much help.

But identifying shorebirds can be easier, and that is what this beginner's guide is all about. Through our user-friendly organization, Color Tab Index, helpful clues, accurate silhouettes, carefully selected photographs, and innovative range and migration maps, you will find it easier and more fun to identify this exciting group of birds. Here are a few additional tips to help you become better acquainted with shorebirds.

Equipment for Watching Shorebirds

Shorebirds are generally located in open spaces and at quite a distance from the observer. They are often stationary or at least moving around in the same area for long periods of time. You need to look closely at the birds, and binoculars are hard to hold steady for long periods and may not be powerful enough to get good looks.

Therefore, having a telescope and tripod can be very important to enjoying and identifying shorebirds. It is also a nice way to take your time. You set up your scope, scan with your binoculars, and then take closer looks at individual birds with the telescope (also called a spotting scope).

How to Start

You will find that people who can identify shorebirds go about it in a manner different from their approach with other kinds of birds. Here are some tips gleaned from their experience.

Take your time — Shorebird identification is a leisurely sport. Generally the birds are in flocks sitting there in front of you, and it is good to set up your telescope and enjoy yourself.

Look over the whole scene — Be sure first to take a brief look at all of the birds in view before trying to identify any one shorebird.

Make some comparisons — As you survey the scene, get a rough idea of how many different kinds of shorebirds are in view by comparing them with each other. How many sizes of birds are there? Are any obviously different from the others? How are they different?

Look for something that you know — If you know any shorebirds, look for one that you know and use it as a "marker bird." A marker bird is one that you can compare in size, shape, color, and behavior with other shorebirds.

Decide if you have a small, medium, *or large shorebird* — Determining size is hard when looking out over a mudflat or beach, but it still can be done through the clues listed inside the front cover of this guide.

Don't identify a shorebird based on one characteristic alone — One characteristic is usually not enough to make a definite identification. It is better to keep adding clues on shape, size, and behavior before clinching your identification.

Learn from experienced birders at that location — People who have watched shorebirds at a given spot will generally know what is usually seen at any particular time. They are a good resource for giving you an idea of what species you are likely to see on that day.

Don't worry if you can't identify them all — Few people can identify all of the shorebirds all of the time. Just start out learning a few, maybe the most common, the largest, or the most distinct. It takes time to learn shorebirds, and they can look very different in new settings or environments or at different times of year.

"Shape and Size Will Be Your Allies"

Because many shorebirds do not have distinctive plumage, especially in winter, one of the best ways to identify a shorebird is through the size and shape of its body and the comparative length of its bill. This book is in part organized on this principle. Here is a summary of ways to tell size, shape, and bill length in shorebirds.

What Size Is It?

When looking across a wide open space dotted with shorebirds, it is often hard to determine the size of the birds, for there are no fixed references. The box on page 15 provides some clues to determining size.

What Shape Is It?

Identifying birds by shape is not something most birdwatchers are used to, since identifying many groups of birds is based largely on plumage color. But shorebird species, especially in non-breeding plumage, can closely resemble each other in coloration, so shape can be a great help in distinguishing them. Actually, shape is important in all bird identification. Here are three things to look for in shorebird shape.

Is the body round and plump or long and thin?
Is the head small or large in relation to the body?
Is the neck long or short?

Is the Bill Short or Long?

When identifying most of the medium-sized shorebirds, determining the length of the bill is important. The best way to determine this is by comparing the length of the bill to the depth of the head. The depth of the head is measured from the base of the bill to the back of the head, or nape. With this comparison you can gauge three different lengths of bills.

Short bill — the bill is noticeably shorter than the depth of the head
Medium bill — the bill is about the depth of the head
Long bill — the bill is clearly much longer than the depth of the head, $1^{1}/_{2}$ to 2 times longer

Large Shorebirds

About the size of a crow, duck, or small gull (like a Ring-billed Gull — a common gull that has a yellow bill with black ring near the tip)

Generally have long legs and long bills

Many have bills distinctive in shape or color

Move more slowly than smaller shorebirds

Medium-sized Shorebirds

About the size of a grackle, robin, or Mourning Dove

Short- or long-legged

Short- or long-billed

Compare with larger and smaller shorebirds

Small Shorebirds

About the size of a swallow or sparrow

About the size of your hand

About the size of one side, or barrel, of your binoculars

Look tiny, move fast, often fidgety

In shallow water or on land

When and Where to Look for Shorebirds

When to Look

Depending on where you are, you can look for shorebirds in any month of the year. The nonbreeding season is a good time to look for shorebirds along the Atlantic, Gulf, and Pacific Coasts because this is where many species spend this time. Shorebirds start gathering on the coasts as early as July and can be seen staying there into early June. Some first-year birds remain all summer on coastal wintering grounds.

During migration, you can look for shorebirds in any of the habitats mentioned below. Remember that migration for shorebirds lasts a long time. For some species, northward migration can start as early as February and continue into June. By this time, some birds have already finished breeding and are starting to migrate south. Southward migration can start in late June and continue into November. This is a wonderfully protracted migration, much longer than in most other groups of birds, and means that there are only about 2 to 3 months of the year when you cannot watch shorebird migration somewhere in North America.

For most species, the breeding period is short, lasting only 1 to 2 months, and occurs in early summer. So if you want to see breeding in shorebirds, you have to get out to their breeding habitats early.

Where to Look

The name "shorebird" masks the tremendous variety of habitats in which you can find these birds nesting, migrating, feeding, and wintering. On the following pages are descriptions of the main habitats in which to see shorebirds and lists of the species that use them.

COASTS

The main times of year when shorebirds can be seen on or near seacoasts are during fall and spring migration and in winter. This is when the birds often gather into huge flocks that settle down to feed and roost. Wintering shorebirds can be seen along the East Coast from Massachusetts to southern Texas and along the West Coast from California north into British Columbia.

Some species also breed along the coasts and can be seen there in midsummer. Other summer coastal shorebirds include the first-year birds of many species that tend to stay on their wintering grounds through their first summer and forgo breeding until their second year.

While most shorebirds prefer sandy or muddy shorelines or salt marshes for feeding, several species are partial to rocky coasts, where they may breed and/or winter.

Shorebirds That Winter on or Near the East Coast

American Avocet	Long-billed Curlew	Short-billed Dowitcher
American Oystercatcher	Long-billed Dowitcher	Snowy Plover
Black-bellied Plover	Marbled Godwit	Solitary Sandpiper
Black-necked Stilt	Piping Plover	Spotted Sandpiper
Dunlin	Purple Sandpiper	Stilt Sandpiper
Greater Yellowlegs	Red Knot	Western Sandpiper
Killdeer	Ruddy Turnstone	Whimbrel
Least Sandpiper	Sanderling	Willet
Lesser Yellowlegs	Semipalmated Plover	Wilson's Plover

Shorebirds That Breed on or Near the East Coast

American Oystercatcher
Black-necked Stilt
Piping Plover
Snowy Plover
Spotted Sandpiper
Willet
Wilson's Plover

Shorebirds That Winter on or Near the West Coast

American Avocet
Black-bellied Plover
Black-necked Stilt
Black Oystercatcher
Black Turnstone
Dunlin
Greater Yellowlegs
Killdeer
Least Sandpiper

Lesser Yellowlegs
Long-billed Curlew
Long-billed Dowitcher
Marbled Godwit
Red Knot
Rock Sandpiper
Ruddy Turnstone
Sanderling
Semipalmated Plover

Short-billed Dowitcher
Snowy Plover
Spotted Sandpiper
Surfbird
Wandering Tattler
Western Sandpiper
Whimbrel
Willet

Shorebirds That Breed on or Near the West Coast

American Avocet
Black-necked Stilt
Black Oystercatcher
Black Turnstone
Snowy Plover
Spotted Sandpiper

Shorebirds That Can Winter and/or Breed on Rocky Coasts

Black Oystercatcher
 (West only)
Black Turnstone
 (West only)

Purple Sandpiper
 (East only)
Rock Sandpiper
 (West only)

Ruddy Turnstone
Surfbird (West only)
Wandering Tattler
 (West only)

PONDS, LAKES, RIVERS

The "shore" in shorebird does not just refer to seashore. The majority of our species have populations that migrate north and/or south through the Midwest, where they can be found along the shores of ponds, lakes, flats, streams, and rivers. This is also true for migrants that migrate inland through eastern or western states. There are also a few species that breed along inland waterways.

Shorebirds That Migrate Through the Midwest and Other Inland States

American Avocet
American Golden-Plover
American Woodcock
Baird's Sandpiper
Black-bellied Plover
Black-necked Stilt
Buff-breasted Sandpiper
   (often in fields)
Common Snipe
Dunlin
Greater Yellowlegs
Hudsonian Godwit
Killdeer

Least Sandpiper
Lesser Yellowlegs
Long-billed Curlew
   (often in fields)
Long-billed Dowitcher
Marbled Godwit
Mountain Plover
   (stays in fields)
Pectoral Sandpiper
Piping Plover
Red-necked Phalarope
Ruddy Turnstone
Semipalmated Plover

Semipalmated Sandpiper
Short-billed Dowitcher
Snowy Plover
Solitary Sandpiper
Spotted Sandpiper
Stilt Sandpiper
Upland Sandpiper
   (stays in fields)
Western Sandpiper
White-rumped Sandpiper
Willet
Wilson's Phalarope

Shorebirds That May Breed on Lakes, Streams, Rivers, or Marshes

American Avocet
Black-necked Stilt
Common Snipe
Piping Plover
Snowy Plover
Spotted Sandpiper
Wandering Tattler
Willet
Wilson's Phalarope

FIELDS, PRAIRIES, WOODS, AND TUNDRA

Several species of shorebirds breed in open short-grass areas such as fields and prairies. Some of these species may never be seen along a shore of any kind. Also there are several species that tend to feed in agricultural fields or grasslands when migrating.

A few shorebirds breed in wooded areas. It is always a little surprising to come across a shorebird in these habitats.

The majority of our shorebirds nest in the tundra of Alaska and northern Canada. Few people get to visit these areas, but if you do and in midsummer, you are likely to encounter nesting shorebirds.

Shorebirds Often Seen in Fields

American Golden-Plover
(nonbreeding only)
American Woodcock
Common Snipe
Buff-breasted Sandpiper
Killdeer
Long-billed Curlew
Marbled Godwit (breeding only)
Mountain Plover
Pacific Golden-Plover
(nonbreeding only)
Upland Sandpiper
Whimbrel (nonbreeding only)

Shorebirds That May Breed in Tundra

American Golden-Plover
Baird's Sandpiper
Bar-tailed Godwit
Black-bellied Plover
Black Turnstone
Buff-breasted Sandpiper
Dunlin
Hudsonian Godwit
Least Sandpiper
Long-billed Dowitcher
Pacific Golden-Plover
Pectoral Sandpiper
Purple Sandpiper

Red Knot
Red-necked Phalarope
Red Phalarope
Rock Sandpiper
Ruddy Turnstone
Sanderling
Semipalmated Plover
Semipalmated Sandpiper
Stilt Sandpiper
Surfbird
Western Sandpiper
Whimbrel
White-rumped Sandpiper

Shorebirds That May Breed in or Near Woods

American Woodcock
Greater Yellowlegs
Lesser Yellowlegs
Solitary Sandpiper
Spotted Sandpiper

Molt and Plumage Variation in Shorebirds

In any group of shorebirds of the same species, you are bound to see a lot of variation in the appearance of their plumage. This is because of several factors, including molt, feather wear, seasonal plumages, and differences between sexes and ages. Having some knowledge of these variations is very helpful when trying to identify shorebirds.

Molt

One type of plumage variation is due to a species having different breeding and nonbreeding plumages. When we see these birds on migration or on their wintering grounds, they may be in various stages of molting from one plumage to the other. (Molting simply means a partial or complete replacement of feathers.)

Most adult shorebirds undergo a complete molt of all their feathers each year from late summer well into fall. Exactly when that molt occurs varies both among and within species. A few species molt before leaving their breeding grounds; many molt during migration; and some molt after completing migration.

Most shorebirds also have some molt in spring, although this does not involve their main flight feathers and usually not their tail. Species that have different summer and winter plumages will molt most of their body feathers at this time.

Juveniles have a slightly different pattern of molt in their first year. They have fresh feathers in late summer, for they are only about a month old. In fall, they molt all of their body feathers (but retain their wing and tail feathers) and grow their first winter plumage, which usually looks much like the adult winter plumage. In spring, they molt most of their body feathers, but keep their original wing and tail feathers and wing coverts. By mid-summer, the wing and tail feathers have become considerably worn and faded. In fall, these birds join the same molt schedule as adults.

Age Differences in Plumage

Differences in age can account for plumage variation. Juveniles in late summer have the freshest and most pristine plumage, while adults will

SEASONAL VARIATION IN PLUMAGE

Twenty of our shorebirds have very different winter and summer plumages; 19 have slight changes; and 10 have no changes. Although assigning the birds to these categories is somewhat subjective, we have provided a list of the species in each category. This information can be useful when learning identification — for those that never change, you only have one plumage to learn.

Very Different Summer and Winter Plumages

American Avocet
American Golden-Plover
Bar-tailed Godwit
Black-bellied Plover
Dunlin
Hudsonian Godwit
Long-billed Dowitcher
Pacific Golden-Plover
Red Knot
Red-necked Phalarope

Red Phalarope
Rock Sandpiper
Ruddy Turnstone
Ruff
Sanderling
Short-billed Dowitcher
Spotted Sandpiper
Wandering Tattler
Willet
Wilson's Phalarope

Slightly Different Summer and Winter Plumages

Baird's Sandpiper
Black Turnstone
Buff-breasted Sandpiper
Greater Yellowlegs
Least Sandpiper
Lesser Yellowlegs
Marbled Godwit
Mountain Plover
Piping Plover
Purple Sandpiper

Semipalmated Plover
Semipalmated Sandpiper
Snowy Plover
Solitary Sandpiper
Stilt Sandpiper
Surfbird
Western Sandpiper
White-rumped Sandpiper
Wilson's Plover

Practically the Same Plumage All Year

American Oystercatcher
American Woodcock
Black-necked Stilt

Black Oystercatcher
Common Snipe
Killdeer

Long-billed Curlew
Solitary Sandpiper

Upland Sandpiper
Whimbrel

look worn, since they have not yet fully molted. Besides looking fresh, juvenal feathers (the first full set of feathers of a young bird) on the back, shoulders, and wing coverts are usually edged with buff, white, reddish brown, or gold, giving the birds a somewhat scaled look.

Birds in their first summer will have wing and tail feathers and wing coverts more worn than those of adults because they have had these same feathers for almost a year. In late summer and fall, adults will look more worn than juveniles, because they have had their feathers longer.

Feather Wear

Another cause of variation is wear. Feathers wear away over the course of the year, and depending on when a bird molts, you will see individuals in various stages of feather condition. Fresh feathers tend to be more richly colored and have lovely neat fringes. Worn feathers are often paler and washed out in appearance and can have very ragged edges. Very worn feathers may even show just the central shaft at the tip.

Sex Differences in Plumage

Marked sexual differences in plumage among North American shorebirds is the exception rather than the rule. For many species there are subtle differences in plumage between the sexes, especially during breeding. And sexual differences in size occur in the majority of our shorebirds, females often being larger than males.

Shorebird Migration

Shorebird migration is one of the most amazing phenomena in the natural world. Perhaps more than any other North American birds, shorebirds are constantly on the move. In fact, many species spend the majority of their lives migrating between their breeding and wintering grounds; some of them, such as the Hudsonian Godwit and the golden-plovers, may cover more than 15,000 miles in a single year (see table on page 26).

In addition to being impressive, the migration of shorebirds is also complex. To help you understand why you see certain shorebirds at certain times, here is a description of each facet of these epic journeys.

Timing

Timing is critical in the migration of shorebirds, many of which are not hardy enough to survive very cold weather. Of the 53 species in this book, most breed in the Arctic, where the summers are very short. Thus, they must mate and raise young in a narrow window of time and depart before the end of summer. Nor can they arrive on the breeding grounds too early, or they will not find enough food.

These timing requirements are the reason the largest numbers of shorebirds are seen migrating in late spring and again in mid- to late summer.

Duration

Despite traveling such amazing distances, shorebirds are not "here today, gone tomorrow"; instead, shorebird migration as a whole is a prolonged event. Depending on where you live in North America, you can observe shorebird migration for up to ten months of the year. In fact, if you have shorebirds wintering in your area, you may notice a sudden expansion of the flock as arriving migrants join them to feed.

"Waves"

In this book, our migration maps show when the first wave of migrants occurs. In the spring, there may be two waves. This happens with species in which one sex goes north first to claim territories, while the other sex migrates as much as three weeks later to begin pairing and breeding. In fall, there may be three waves: adults leave before juveniles, and in most species, one sex takes no part in raising young and therefore can leave the breeding grounds before the other sex.

Staging

In the course of their travels, shorebirds must make long pauses at food-rich locations to build up their energy through days of nonstop feeding. This is known as staging, and the locations are called staging areas. Staging is critical in migration, since weak, underfed birds will fail to reach their destinations. Some species are more dependent on staging sites than others and will stage longer. Those species generally have a more prolonged migration period.

Several staging areas in North America are of critical importance to shorebirds. These sites can host tens of thousands, even hundreds of thousands, of birds. In fact, most North American shorebird migrants pass through at least one of these areas.

Copper River Delta, Alaska
Kachemak Bay, Alaska
Mono Lake, California
Salton Sea, California
San Francisco Bay, California
Cheyenne Bottoms, Kansas
Duson/Crowley, Louisiana
Lahontan Valley, Nevada
Delaware Bay, New Jersey
Devils Lake, North Dakota
Quill Lakes, Saskatchewan
Bolivar Flats, Texas
Brazoria National Wildlife Refuge, Texas
Laguna Atascosa National Wildlife Refuge, Texas
Great Salt Lake, Utah
Grays Harbor, Washington

MIGRATION DISTANCE

The distances traveled by shorebirds vary widely according to species. Here is a breakdown of North American shorebirds according to one-way migration distance.

Long Distance (average trip of more than 8,000 miles)

American Golden-Plover
Baird's Sandpiper
Buff-breasted Sandpiper
Hudsonian Godwit
Pacific Golden-Plover
Pectoral Sandpiper
Stilt Sandpiper
White-rumped Sandpiper

Medium Distance (average trip of about 3,500 to 7,500 miles)

Bar-tailed Godwit
Black-bellied Plover
Black Turnstone
Dunlin
Greater Yellowlegs
Least Sandpiper
Lesser Yellowlegs
Long-billed Dowitcher
Purple Sandpiper
Red Knot
Red-necked Phalarope
Red Phalarope
Ruddy Turnstone
Ruff
Sanderling
Semipalmated Plover
Semipalmated Sandpiper
Short-billed Dowitcher
Solitary Sandpiper
Spotted Sandpiper
Surfbird
Upland Sandpiper
Wandering Tattler
Western Sandpiper
Whimbrel
Wilson's Phalarope

Short Distance (average trip of less than 3,000 miles)

American Avocet
American Oyster-catcher
American Woodcock
Black-necked Stilt
Common Snipe
Killdeer
Long-billed Curlew
Marbled Godwit
Mountain Plover
Piping Plover
Rock Sandpiper
Snowy Plover
Willet
Wilson's Plover

Nonmigratory

Black Oystercatcher

Shorebird Conservation

Shorebird conservation today is focusing on several interrelated issues: declining populations, threats to vital migration stopover locations, and the effects of human disturbance.

Key Issues

Declining Populations

Recent studies of shorebird populations have shown serious declines in the populations of several species, including Black-bellied Plover, Mountain Plover, Whimbrel, Sanderling, Semipalmated Sandpiper, Least Sandpiper, Stilt Sandpiper, and Short-billed Dowitcher. Many other species are suspected to have declining populations, but information from surveys is still lacking. The reasons for their declines are not clear, but human development of staging areas and breeding sites is among them.

Critical Staging Areas

Because shorebirds are some of our most long-distance migrants, often traveling thousands of miles each spring and fall, refueling places along their journey are essential to their survival. Critical staging areas are often few and far between on the shorebirds' journeys. The birds count on them as a place to rest, feed, and build up the fat reserves they need for the next leg of their journey.

These stopover areas are under attack by human encroachment, and this can quickly affect the shorebirds and their populations. These sites have been used by the shorebirds for centuries, and in many cases the birds simply do not have alternative places to feed. Without their critical staging areas they could perish. Attempts are being made to delineate these sites, and more steps need to be taken to protect them.

Human Disturbance to Shoreline Breeding Habitats

Several species of shorebirds nest along lakeshores or on the seacoast. There is a direct conflict between their needs and the desire of humans for summer recreation in these same areas. In many cases, sharing of the same habitat can occur if there is sensitivity on the part of humans to the needs of the birds and the timing of their breeding.

One key issue is the driving of vehicles along beaches. This affects the birds in a variety of ways. It directly destroys eggs and nests as the cars or buggies drive over them. It can scare the parents off a nest, leaving the eggs and/or young vulnerable to predators, like gulls, in the area. In addition, the tire tracks resulting from the use of vehicles on sand or mud can be deep, and sometimes these trap just-hatched shorebirds that cannot get out of them.

With sensitivity and education, people and shorebirds can share these habitats, benefiting the birds and enriching our human lives.

What You Can Do

Reduce Disturbance of Wintering and Migrating Shorebirds

Shorebirds on wintering grounds and at stopover sites on migration need to maintain their health and build fat reserves for migration. It is critical that we not disturb them during these times. The main way we can help is by observing these points:

♦ Never chase flocks of shorebirds.
♦ Never let dogs chase shorebirds.
♦ Stop other people's children and dogs from chasing shorebirds, and explain to them why this is so important.

The birds are often tired, thin, hungry, and possibly even weak from their long journeys. Any extra disturbance or causing them to take flight costs them energy and prevents them from making the most of the short times they have to feed. Getting food in the wild is never easy. Letting the shorebirds feed in peace is one of the best conservation measures we can take.

Become Active in Shorebird Conservation

Many of the species that appear on the following pages are in decline because of habitat destruction and desperately need our help to recover. As we discussed earlier, shorebirds depend heavily on staging areas, where they fuel up for their long flights. Despite extensive study of the subject, gaps remain in our knowledge of where shorebirds are stopping over. By participating as an observer and keeping track of migrant shorebirds coming through your local areas, you can help fill these gaps, allowing more staging areas to be identified and preserved. In this way, you can help stop the decline in shorebird populations.

In 1974, Manomet Center for Conservation Sciences, in Massachusetts, organized the International Shorebird Survey (ISS) to gather information on shorebirds, their populations, and the habitats they use. Relying mostly on skilled volunteer observers, the ISS has gathered over 42,000 censuses with more than 900 observers participating.

The Western Hemisphere Shorebird Reserve Network, a coalition of more than 120 public and private agencies in seven countries throughout North and South America, was formed in 1986 to monitor shorebird populations and determine critical areas for shorebird conservation.

Both these cooperative efforts are crucial to gathering further information on the status of shorebirds in the Western Hemisphere. Without baseline information on the status of any species of wildlife, we cannot gauge over time how well that species is faring. All of us need to support these efforts with contributions of our time and resources.

If you would like to get involved, keep a count of each shorebird species you see, and where and when you see it. Submit your results to the International Shorebird Survey. For more information, contact ISS director Brian Harrington, c/o Manomet Bird Observatory, Box 1770, Manomet, MA 02345.

Resources on Shorebirds

Organizations

Biological Resources Division, U.S.
Geological Survey
Midcontinent Ecological Science
Center
Fort Collins, CO 80525-3400
Internet: http://www.mesc.usgs.gov/
shorebirds

International Shorebird Survey
c/o Manomet Bird Observatory
Brian Harrington, Director
Box 1770
Tel. 508-224-6521; Fax 508-224-9220
Manomet, MA 02345
Internet: http://www.im.nbs.gov/iss/
iss.html

U.S. Fish & Wildlife Service
Division of Migratory Bird
Management
Washington, DC 20240
Internet: http://migratorybirds.fws.
gov/shrbird/shrbird.html

Western Hemisphere Shorebird
Reserve Network (WHSRN)
c/o Manomet Bird Observatory
Box 1770
Manomet, MA 02345
Internet: http://www.manomet.org/
WHSRN.htm

Books

Bent, Arthur Cleveland. *Life Histories of North American Shorebirds.* Parts one and two. New York: Dover Publications, 1962.
Dickinson, Mary, ed. *National Geographic Field Guide to the Birds of North America.* Third edition. Washington, D.C.: National Geographic Society, 1999.
Hayman, Peter, John Marchant, and Tony Prater. *Shorebirds: An Identification Guide.* Boston: Houghton Mifflin Company, 1986.
Paulson, Dennis. *Shorebirds of the Pacific Northwest.* Seattle: University of Washington Press, 1993.

Acknowledgments

Poole, Alan, and Frank Gill, eds. *The Birds of North America.* Philadelphia: Academy of Natural Sciences, 1992–2000.

Stokes, Donald and Lillian. *Stokes Field Guide to Birds: Eastern Region.* Boston: Little, Brown, 1996.

———. *Stokes Field Guide to Birds: Western Region.* Boston: Little, Brown, 1996.

Terres, John. *The Audubon Society Encyclopedia of North American Birds.* New York: Wings Books, 1991.

Zimmer, Kevin. *Birding in the American West: A Handbook.* Ithaca, N.Y.: Cornell University Press, 2000.

We would like to give special thanks to several people who were of tremendous help in creating this guide to shorebirds.

Brian Harrington at Manomet Center for Conservation Sciences has been a leader in shorebird research, education, and conservation for decades, and he generously made available the prepublication draft of "An Atlas of Shorebird Migration in the Contiguous 48 States of the United States," compiled by Brian A. Harrington and Laura X. Payne. This is, in part, a summary of the information collected by the International Shorebird Survey from 1974 to 1996 and was used as the basis for our shorebird migration maps. We also thank him for going over our maps and giving us input and encouragement.

Alan Poole of the Philadelphia Academy of Natural Sciences kindly sent us prepublication drafts of shorebird accounts that will appear in the spectacular work called *The Birds of North America,* of which he is the managing editor. This is a superb series of monographs on all species of North American birds, and we have used its information to help in the writing of this guide.

Simon Perkins, ornithologist for the Massachusetts Audubon Society, has been kind enough to help us pick the best photographs to illustrate the most important plumages for each species and to check on their accuracy.

Michael O'Brien, Richard Crossley, and Kevin Karlson read over the final manuscript and made careful corrections and additions, for which we are grateful. A special thanks to Michael and Richard for their clues on distinguishing Long-billed and Short-billed Dowitchers in winter plumage.

And finally, Tom Young, our assistant in our office, has helped us in many ways to make this a better guide, not the least of which was gathering the information for and making the migration and distribution maps.

Of course, we take full responsibility for any errors that may have inadvertently slipped by us during production of this work. We hope this guide is useful to birders at all levels of expertise and that it furthers the conservation and enjoyment of shorebirds.

Don and Lillian Stokes

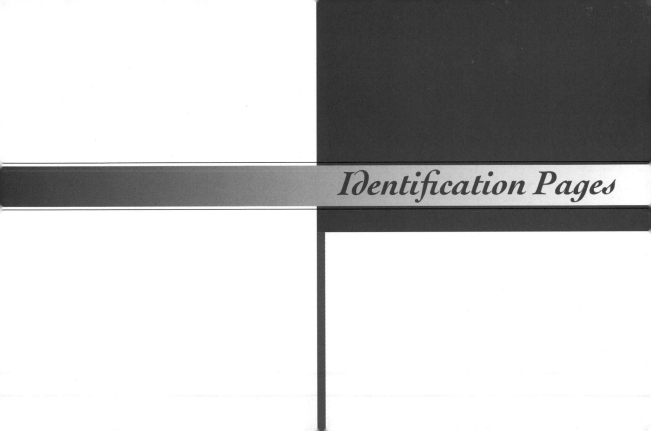

Identification Pages

Large shorebirds are some of the easiest to identify, for each has something very distinctive about it. Below are the distinctive features with the birds that have them.

Our only large shorebird with very long bright yellow legs: Greater Yellowlegs, p. 38.

Greater Yellowlegs 14"

Large grayish shorebird with striking black-and-white pattern on opened wings (wing pattern is hidden when bird lands): Willet, p. 36.

Willet 15"

Good Marker Bird

American Avocet 18"

Thin sharply upturned bill: American Avocet, p. 42.

Black-necked Stilt 14"

Extremely long bubblegum-pink legs: Black-necked Stilt, p. 40.

34

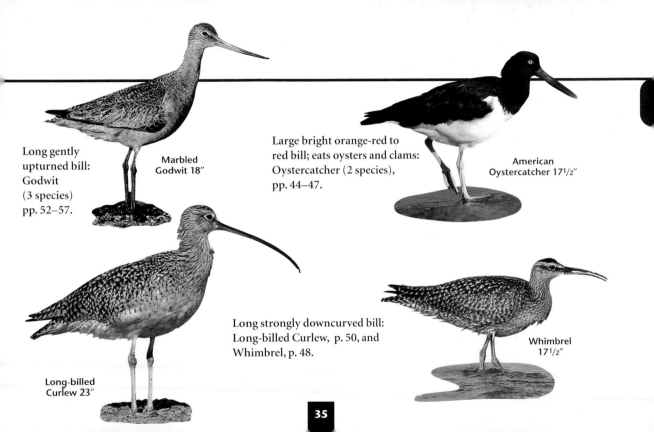

Long gently upturned bill: Godwit (3 species) pp. 52–57.

Marbled Godwit 18″

Large bright orange-red to red bill; eats oysters and clams: Oystercatcher (2 species), pp. 44–47.

American Oystercatcher 17½″

Long strongly downcurved bill: Long-billed Curlew, p. 50, and Whimbrel, p. 48.

Long-billed Curlew 23″

Whimbrel 17½″

Willet
Catoptrophorus semipalmatus, 15"

Main Year-round Clues

Large heavily built shorebird. Legs long, thick, and gray. Bill thick, grayish at base, darker at tip. See In Flight.

Additional Summer Clues

Grayish or mottled brown upper parts. Dark streaking on neck and dark barring on breast and flanks.

Additional Winter Clues

Smooth gray above; whitish below.

Juvenile Clues

Like winter adult but browner, with pale edges to back and wing feathers.

In Flight

Bold white wing-stripe on black wings is striking and an easy clue.

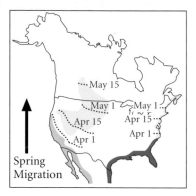

Separate East and West Coast migrations involve two different subspecies.

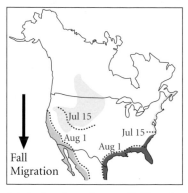

Interior breeders migrate to Gulf, southern Atlantic, or southern Pacific coast. Coastal breeders leave the country.

Call

A loud rolling "poor will willet."

Summer adult, western race (*inornatus*)

Summer adult, eastern race (*semipalmatus*)

Winter adult

In flight

Greater Yellowlegs
Tringa melanoleuca, 14″

Main Year-round Clues
A graceful, grayish shorebird. Legs long, bright yellow to orange. Bill long, thin; about 1½ times length of head; may appear slightly upturned. (Lesser Yellowlegs, p. 74, has bill that is finer and straight and about same length as head.)

Additional Summer Clues
Neck and head strongly streaked. Flanks have dark barring.

Additional Winter Clues
Head and neck lightly streaked. Flanks white or only faintly barred. Bill usually gray at base.

In Flight
No wing-stripe; white rump.

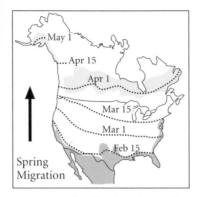

Migrates north earlier than does similar Lesser Yellowlegs. Most common at coastal sites, especially salt marshes.

Call
Three or more loud downslurred whistles; last note usually lower and more downslurred, like "tee tee teer."

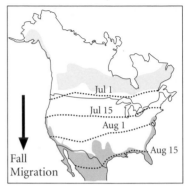

Migration lasts longer than that of Lesser Yellowlegs; migrants seen well into November. In interior, less common than in spring.

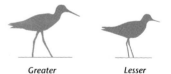

Greater   **Lesser**

Note difference between Greater and Lesser Yellowlegs in relative length of bill and overall size.

Summer adult

Molting adult

Lesser (left) and Greater (right) Yellowlegs for size comparison

Black-necked Stilt
Himantopus mexicanus, 14"

Main Year-round Clues

Legs extremely long, bubblegum-pink.
Black above; white below. Bill all black,
long, needlelike. On male, back is black;
on female, back is very dark brown.

In Flight

Black above except for white rump and tail
and white wedge up back. Long pink legs
extend well beyond tail.

Call

Loud "kek kek kek."

*A few spring migrants temporarily over-
shoot breeding range, to New Jersey in
east and British Columbia in west.*

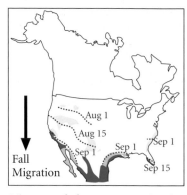

*Migrants make long stops at staging sites
but tend to bypass Carolinas. Mostly
seen wading in deep water.*

Adult male

Adult female

Flock in flight

41

American Avocet
Recurvirostra americana, 18"

Main Year-round Clues
Long, very thin, upturned bill. Striking black-and-white pattern on wings and back. Legs long, gray. Female has shorter, more strongly upturned bill than male.

Additional Summer Clues
Head and neck rich cinnamon.

Additional Winter Clues
Head and neck grayish white.

In Flight
Bold pattern of black and white on back.

Call
A loud penetrating "kleeet."

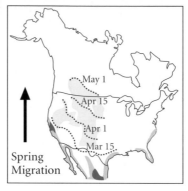

Spring Migration

Migration paths and timing vary somewhat from year to year. May begin migrating as early as February.

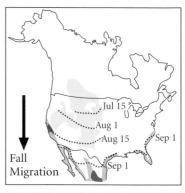

Fall Migration

Individuals may band together in groups of thousands before migrating. Rare in east from New Jersey to New England.

Summer adult male

Winter adult female

In flight

Main Year-round Clues

Large, heavyset, black-and-white shorebird with a bright orange-red bill. Head and neck black, back brown, underparts white. Bill long, bright orange-red, heavy, but laterally narrow. Legs thick, dull yellow to flesh-colored. Eye yellow with orange-red ring around it. One-to-two-year-old birds have dull orange-brown bill with dark tip.

In Flight

Bold white wing-stripes on black wings. White rump and black tail. Typical flight is low with bowed wings.

Call

Loud slightly ascending whistles: "wheeep wheeep"; also long rising and descending whistles.

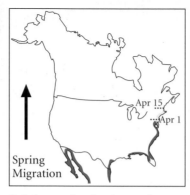

Strictly coastal, on beaches or salt marsh. Northward migration is rapid but poorly documented.

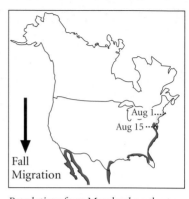

Populations from Maryland north move south in fall. Populations from Virginia south are nonmigratory residents.

Adult

Flock

Juvenile

Black Oystercatcher
Haematopus bachmani, 17½"

Non-migratory

Largely nonmigratory, though slightly less widespread in winter; some birds move short distances to winter feeding areas.

Main Year-round Clues
Large, heavyset, all-black shorebird with a bright red bill. Bill long, bright red, and heavy but laterally narrow. Legs thick and dull yellow to flesh-colored. Eye yellow with orange-red ring around it. One-to-two-year-old birds have dull orange-brown bill with dark tip.

In Flight
All black. Typical flight is low with bowed wings.

Call
Loud piping whistles, like "wheeep wheeep."

Adult

Whimbrel
Numenius phaeopus, 17½"

Main Year-round Clues
Large-bodied brown shorebird with a long downcurved bill. Two wide dark stripes on crown. Bill less than half the body length; lower mandible can be pinkish at base. Legs blue-gray and relatively short. Plumage about the same all year.

In Flight
Underwings buffy; belly pale.

Call
Rapidly repeated short whistles, like "whi-whi-whi-whi-whi-whi"; often given in flight.

Most migrants from Mid-Atlantic fly nonstop to Hudson Bay. Eastern and western populations are separate.

Common in New England, although sparse there in spring. Migrants often gather into huge, spectacular nocturnal roosts.

Juvenile

Worn summer adult

Marbled Godwit
Limosa fedoa, 18"

Main Year-round Clues

Large shorebird with a long gently upturned bill. Cinnamon overall; mottled with black above; variable black barring underneath. Legs long, gray. Bill pink to orange at base, darker at tip. Winter and summer plumage similar, but more barred underneath in summer.

In Flight

Appearance is cinnamon above and below, with darker wing tips. No wing-stripe.

Call

Calls during breeding are "gaweet gaweet"; often given in flight.

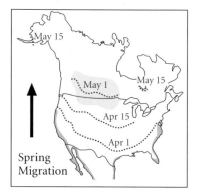

Spring Migration

Massive flocks of migrants (up to 200,000) may congregate at Great Salt Lake. Rare on Northeast Coast.

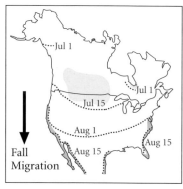

Fall Migration

Usually seen on intertidal flats of bays or rivers. Regular on Northeast Coast, though not numerous.

Summer adult

Worn adult

In flight

Hudsonian Godwit
Limosa haemastica, 15½"

Main Year-round Clues
Large shorebird with a long gently
upturned bill. Distinctive in flight; see In
Flight. Legs long, dark gray to black. Bill
pink to orange at base, darker at tip.

Additional Summer Clues
Body brown above; dark reddish below,
with varied amounts of darker barring.
Male is darker red beneath and more
spotted above than female.

Additional Winter Clues
Unstreaked dark gray head, neck, and back.
Pale gray belly.

In Flight
White rump; dark tail; white wing-stripe
above. Dark underwing coverts distinctive.

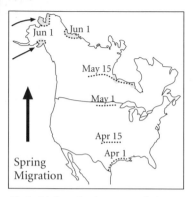

Jun 1   Jun 1

May 15

May 1

Apr 15

Apr 1

Spring
Migration

*Alaska birds arrive from Australasia.
Northwest Territories birds are most
likely from main interior migration.*

Jul 1

Jul 15

Aug 1

Aug 15

Fall
Migration

*Migration mainly nonstop over Atlantic
to South America; migrants uncommon
on East Coast. Alaska birds to
Australasia.*

Call
Common call is "kaweep kaweep."

Summer male

Summer female

Adult molting to winter plumage

In flight

Bar-tailed Godwit
Limosa lapponica, 16"

Main Year-round Clues
Large shorebird with a long gently upturned bill. Shorter legs and shorter bill than other godwits. Greater primary extension than Marbled Godwit (p. 52).

Additional Summer Clues
Male bright unbarred rufous-orange below. Female slightly larger and paler below.

Additional Winter Clues
Streaked gray head, neck, and back. Pale belly. More distinct eyebrow than Marbled Godwit.

In Flight
Dark barring on tail. Wings gray beneath.

Call
Calls "key key keya"; often given in flight.

Spring Migration

Favors tidal edges in migration. Occasionally also seen at inland wetlands.

Fall Migration

Rare vagrant on Pacific and Atlantic Coasts, including in winter. Winters in southern Asia and Australia.

56

Summer male

Summer female

Juvenile

BIRDS WITH BILLS TWICE AS LONG AS HEAD

Dowitchers feed in water, rapidly probing in sewing-machine fashion. Bills of these two species overlap in size, making bill length a usable clue only at the extremes of short or long.

Long-billed Dowitcher flight call is a high-pitched "kwik" or "keek"; often found in freshwater marshes. P. 66.

Long-billed Dowitcher 11½"

Short-billed Dowitcher flight call is a mellow "tututu"; often found in coastal and saltwater marshes. P. 64.

Short-billed Dowitcher 11"

Woodcock and snipe feed on land; generally prefer muddy and moist areas.

American Woodcock has a dark back with no stripes; rounded wings in flight. Found in fields and woods. P. 70.

American Woodcock 11"

Common Snipe has a dark back with conspicuous white stripes; pointed wings in flight. Found in wet meadows and marsh edges. P. 68.

Common Snipe 10½"

BIRDS WITH BILLS ABOUT 1½ TIMES AS LONG AS HEAD

Dunlin and Stilt Sandpiper both have long slightly downcurved bills and feed in a manner similar to dowitchers — rapidly probing their bill into deeper water sewing-machine fashion. The Dunlin is a very common and widespread shorebird; the Stilt Sandpiper is uncommon and limited in range.

Good Marker Bird

Dunlin 8½″

Summer

Winter

Stilt Sandpiper 8½″

Dunlin is a rotund, short-necked shorebird, common of mudflats, where it is often seen in large flocks. In winter it is plain gray above with a gray breast and white belly; in summer it has a black belly patch and is reddish brown above. Legs are dark gray to black. P. 60.

Stilt Sandpiper is a sleek, long-necked, and long-legged shorebird; legs are greenish yellow. P. 62.

Dunlin
Calidris alpina, 8½"

Main Year-round Clues
A small plump shorebird with a relatively small head and short neck. Bill black, relatively long, droops at the tip; "drooping Dunlin." Legs dark gray to black. Feeds with bill rapidly probing into water. Often in large winter flocks that periodically fly up in beautiful coordinated flights.

Additional Summer Clues
Face and underparts whitish; large black patch on belly. Back and scapulars bright reddish brown; crown variably streaked.

Additional Winter Clues
Upperparts and breast plain gray. Belly and undertail coverts all white.

Spring Migration

Three distinct migration paths. West Coast subspecies migrates to Alaska only; central and western populations do not mingle.

In Flight
Narrow white wing-stripe; dark central tail feathers.

Call
Flight call is a raspy "zree."

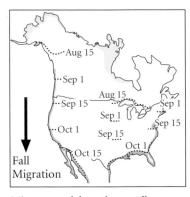

Fall Migration

Migrates much later than small sandpipers. Often seen in large flocks of hundreds to thousands of birds, all in synchronized flight.

Dunlin   **Stilt Sandpiper**   **Western Sandpiper**

Stilt and Western Sandpipers have a bill shape similar to Dunlin's, but their overall silhouettes are distinctive.

Summer adult

Winter adult

Molting adult

In flight

Stilt Sandpiper
Calidris himantopus, 8½"

Main Year-round Clues
A medium-sized, graceful, long-necked, long-legged shorebird. Bill long, black, slightly drooped at tip. Legs long, greenish yellow. Feeds in deep water with rapid probing motions, often submerging head.

Additional Summer Clues
Ear patch reddish brown; eyebrow white, distinct. Head and neck with dark streaking. Breast, belly, and undertail coverts strongly barred. Back feathers dark brown, edged with rufous and white. Wing coverts are a contrasting unmarked brown.

Additional Winter Clues
Grayish above; whitish below; wing feathers edged with white. Breast finely streaked. Undertail coverts spotted.

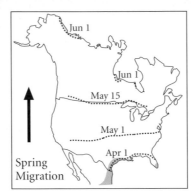

Most take central path, fly nonstop from Kansas to upper Midwest. From Virginia, migrants head inland to Hudson Bay.

In Flight
No wing-stripes; rump white in winter, mottled grayish in summer.

Call
Flight call a soft "tooo" or a short flat "chirrt" given mostly in winter and migration.

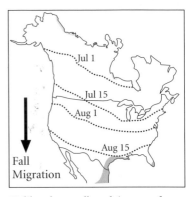

Unlike other small sandpipers, prefers feeding in belly-deep water. More widespread than in spring, especially juveniles.

Summer adult

Adult molting to winter plumage

Juvenile molting into first winter plumage

In flight

63

Limnodromus griseus, 11"

Main Year-round Clues

Medium-sized plump shorebird. Bill very long, straight, dark. Legs grayish green. Call is a mellow "tututu." Most often in coastal and saltwater areas.

Additional Summer Clues

Eastern and western subspecies have white on belly; orange neck with heavy or dense spotting. Midwest subspecies has orange belly and neck with little or no white on belly; dark spots on breast. Compare with Long-billed Dowitcher, p. 66.

Additional Winter Clues

Pale gray breast with fine speckles; thin, sharply defined flank bars on white background; back and scapulars uniform pale gray. Compare with Long-billed Dowitcher.

Two distinct migration paths. Western subspecies geographically separate from two eastern subspecies.

In Flight

Dark wings with no wing-stripe. White stripe up back.

Call

Flight call is a mellow "tututu"; lower-pitched than call of Long-billed Dowitcher.

Moves south earlier than similar Long-billed Dowitcher. Most E. Coast migrants fly nonstop from Mid-Atlantic to S. Am.

Dowitcher   **Dunlin**   **Black-bellied Plover**

Dowitchers and Dunlin have similar silhouettes, but Dunlin is smaller. Compare size with Black-bellied Plover.

Summer adult

Adult molting

Winter adult

Juvenile

Long-billed Dowitcher
Limnodromus scolopaceus, 11½"

Main Year-round Clues
Medium-sized plump shorebird. Bill very long, straight, dark. Legs grayish green. Call is a sharp "kwik" or "keek." Most often in freshwater areas. Overlap in bill size with Short-billed Dowitcher makes this trait less useful as an identifier.

Additional Summer Clues
Underparts entirely reddish brown. Narrow dark brown and white barring on breast and flanks. No white on belly.

Additional Winter Clues
Smooth dark gray breast contrasts sharply with white belly; thick, smudgy dark flank bars on gray background; back and scapulars have dark gray centers fading to paler edges. Compare with Short-billed Dowitcher (p. 64).

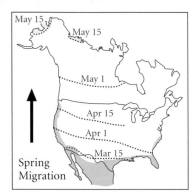

Spring Migration

Moves north earlier, and more common in interior states, than Short-billed Dowitcher. Few seen in eastern states.

In Flight
Wings all dark with no wing-stripe. White stripe up back.

Call
Flight call is a sharp "kwik" or "keek"; higher-pitched than call of Short-billed Dowitcher. Can be given in a rapid series, "kikikikik."

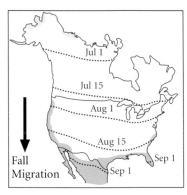

Fall Migration

Lingers longer into fall than does Short-billed Dowitcher; many migrants seen in November.

Dowitcher   Dunlin   Black-bellied Plover

Dowitchers and Dunlin have similar silhouettes, but Dunlin is smaller. Compare size with Black-bellied Plover.

Summer adult

Winter adult

Juvenile

In flight

67

Common Snipe
Gallinago gallinago, 10½"

Main Year-round Clues

A medium-sized plump shorebird with a very long bill. Back dark with conspicuous light stripes. Head boldly patterned with dark and light stripes. Legs short and greenish yellow. Usually seen in wet meadows, pond edges, and marshes.

In Flight

Flies in a characteristic zigzag manner. Wings pointed at tips; wings rounded in similar American Woodcock (p. 70). No white stripe up back as in dowitchers (pp. 64, 66).

Call

A nasal "scaip." On breeding ground gives a "wheet wheet" call and a whinnying sound in flight display.

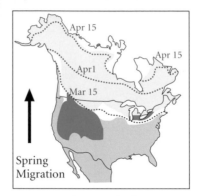

Spring Migration

Migrates north primarily after warm fronts. Seen mostly in wet fields or marshes; sometimes along streams or ponds.

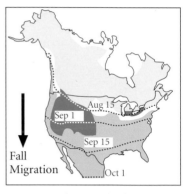

Fall Migration

Migrates south primarily after cold fronts. Usually seen in flocks of various sizes when feeding.

Dowitcher

Common Snipe

Snipe has shorter neck and legs than similar dowitcher.

Adult

American Woodcock
Scolopax minor, 11"

Main Year-round Clues

A medium-sized plump shorebird with a very long bill. Bill pale gray or brown at base; darker at tip. Eyes noticeably large and dark. Head larger and neck shorter than in Common Snipe. Back dark with no light stripes; breast buffy. Usually seen in woods or forest edges (rarely marshes).

In Flight

Wings rounded at tips; Common Snipe (p. 68) has pointed wings. Makes clattering sound with wings when flushed. Does circling display flights high in the air over breeding grounds at dusk.

Call

On breeding grounds gives a buzzy nasal "peeent" from the ground and a songbird-like chirping during aerial displays.

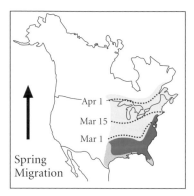

Spring Migration

Apr 1
Mar 15
Mar 1

Timing of both migrations extremely variable and heavily influenced by weather; in spring, triggered by warm fronts.

Fall Migration

Sep 1
Sep 15
Oct 1
Oct 15

Inconspicuous during movement south; usually seen skulking along forest floor or in flight at dusk. Migration period prolonged.

American Woodcock   Common Snipe

Note shorter legs and neck and larger head of American Woodcock when compared with similar Common Snipe.

Adult

The shorebirds in this group are varied. Some can be recognized by habitat, others by a physical trait, others by behavior. Look through the clues to narrow your choices for identification and then turn to the species description on the page indicated.

Yellowlegs are the only shorebirds with long bright yellow legs. Compare Lesser Yellowlegs (p. 74) with Greater Yellowlegs (p. 38) for overall size and for size of bill in proportion to head.

Pectoral Sandpiper has a yellowish bill and heavy streaking on its breast which stops abruptly at its belly, creating a bib effect. P. 78.

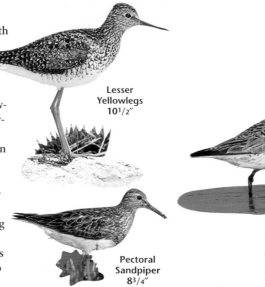

Lesser Yellowlegs
10¹/₂"

Pectoral Sandpiper
8³/₄"

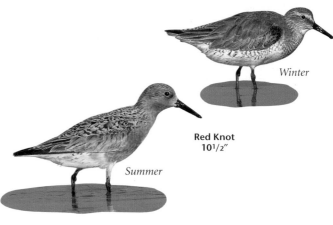

Winter

Red Knot
10¹/₂"

Summer

Red Knot is a small-headed, medium-billed, dumpy, plump shorebird. Red breast in summer. In winter the Red Knot is "not red." Often in large flocks. P. 76.

Rocky Shore Birds

Birds found usually on rocky shores include the similar Purple Sandpiper (shown) and Rock Sandpiper. Both mostly seen in winter. Purple (p. 80) is in East, Rock (p. 82) is in West.

Purple
Sandpiper 9"

"Bobbers"

The Solitary Sandpiper repeatedly bobs the front of its body; it has a dark back and white eye-ring. Often seen alone. P. 84. See also Spotted Sandpiper, p. 140.

Solitary
Sandpiper
8½"

Wandering Tattler repeatedly bobs its tail as it feeds in winter along rocky West Coast. A stocky gray bird with short, dull yellow legs. P. 86.

Wandering
Tattler 11"

Ruff's Rare

The Ruff is a rare shorebird with a small head and large body. Juvenal and winter plumages most often seen. P. 94.

Ruff 9–11"

Swim in Circles

Phalaropes typically swim about in circles as they feed in deeper water and pick prey off the upper layer. They are small thin-billed birds with longish necks. Of the three species, Wilson's Phalarope (shown) is more often seen; other two stay more in ocean. Pp. 88–93.

Wilson's
Phalarope
9¼"

Summer female

Lesser Yellowlegs
Tringa flavipes, 10½″

Main Year-round Clues

A graceful grayish shorebird. Legs long, bright yellow to orange. Bill straight, thin; about same length as head. (Greater Yellowlegs, p. 38, has bill about 1½ times length of head.)

Additional Summer Clues

Neck and head strongly streaked. Flanks with thin black barring. (Less heavily barred than Greater Yellowlegs.)

Additional Winter Clues

Head and neck lightly streaked. Flanks white. Bill all black. (Greater Yellowlegs often has gray at base of bill in winter.)

In Flight

No wing-stripe; white rump.

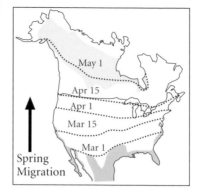

Main route is through midcontinent west of Mississippi River; occurs in low numbers elsewhere.

Call

One to three soft downslurred notes, like "tew tew."

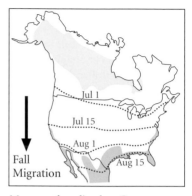

Moves south earlier than Greater Yellowlegs. Usually in flocks of 3–25, on mudflats with dowitchers and other shorebirds.

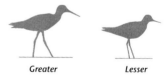

Greater   Lesser

Note difference between Lesser and Greater Yellowlegs in relative length of bill and overall size and shape.

Summer adult

Winter

Juvenile

Red Knot
Calidris canutus, 10½"

Main Year-round Clues
A medium-sized plump-looking shorebird. Bill looks short, about the length of its head. Legs vary from dark gray to olive-yellow. Often seen in large flocks. Strong seasonal differences in plumage.

Additional Summer Clues
Obvious brick-red neck and breast.

Additional Winter Clues
Grayish and plain with very few distinctive features; if it is "not" any other shorebird, it is often a "Knot." Note size and relatively small head in relation to body size.

In Flight
Generally gray above; wing-stripe is thin; rump is mottled gray and white; tail is light gray.

Spring Migration

Two separate migration paths. Migrants form vast flocks with Ruddy Turnstones and Sanderlings at Delaware Bay.

Call
Generally quiet in flight, but may give a soft "kuret."

Fall Migration

In East, less common than in spring, as many birds fly nonstop from Hudson Bay to South America.

Red Knot   Dunlin   Sanderling

These birds have similar silhouettes. Note differences in bill length relative to head length and head size relative to body size.

Summer adult

Adult molting into summer plumage

Winter adult

Juvenile

Main Year-round Clues

A stocky, short-legged, small-headed shorebird. Dense brown streaking on breast ends abruptly at white belly. Bill all black or with paler yellowish base, slightly downturned at tip. Legs yellowish green. Often feeds in muddy or marshy areas away from other shorebirds. Male is larger and darker-breasted than female.

Juvenile Clues

Feathers on back are fringed with buff or white. Broader white edges on back feathers form two white V's on back. Juvenile generally similar to adult.

In Flight

Faint wing-stripe. Dark central tail feathers.

May 15
May 1
Apr 15
Apr 1
Mar 15
Mar 1

Spring Migration

Most migrants in interior, between Mississippi River and Rocky Mountains; few in East. Seen in grassy wetlands or agricultural fields.

Call

Flight call is a low "churk."

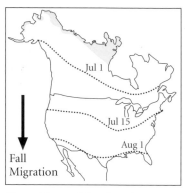

Jul 1
Jul 15
Aug 1

Fall Migration

More widespread than in spring; juveniles seen in coastal states, often with golden-plovers, Buff-breasted Sandpipers.

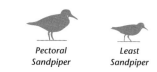

Pectoral Sandpiper   Least Sandpiper

These two have similar silhouettes. Note Pectoral's very small head in relation to body size.

Summer adult female

Juvenile

Purple Sandpiper
Calidris maritima, 9"

Main Year-round Clues

A dark plump shorebird, seen mostly in winter along eastern rocky coasts. Bill orangish yellow at base, relatively long, slightly drooped at tip. Legs short, orangish yellow.

Additional Summer Clues

Crown brownish. Head and neck with dark streaking. Breast and flanks with dark spots. Scapulars black with rufous or gold edges.

Additional Winter Clues

Upperparts dark grayish. Belly white with large gray spots.

In Flight

Narrow white wing-stripe. Dark tail and central rump feathers, white on sides of rump.

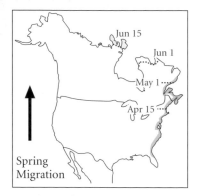

Occurs on rocks at edge of crashing waves, often on breakwaters. Most wintering birds linger into May before departing.

Call

Flight call is a "weeet" or a "whititit whit."

Gregarious; almost always seen in flocks, sometimes with Ruddy Turnstones. Accidental in Great Lakes region and on Gulf Coast.

Summer adult

Winter adult

Winter flock in flight

Rock Sandpiper
Calidris ptilocnemis, 9"

Main Year-round Clues
A plump shorebird, seen mostly on western coastal rocky shores. Bill orangish yellow at base, relatively long, slightly drooped at tip. Legs short and greenish yellow. Very similar to Purple Sandpiper (p. 80).

Additional Summer Clues
Black patch on belly. Crown and back feathers black with reddish-brown edges. Base of bill is usually yellowish.

Additional Winter Clues
Clear dark gray upperparts. Spotting on breast continues along flanks and onto white belly.

In Flight
Narrow white wing-stripe. Grayish tail; dark central rump feathers; white on sides of rump.

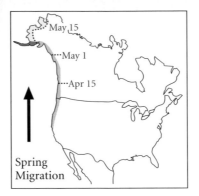

Habitat and behavior identical to those of Purple Sandpiper. Migration fairly rapid; migration period brief.

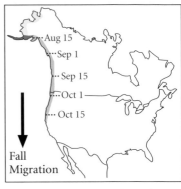

Usually in flocks; often with Black Turnstones and Surfbirds. Very rarely seen inland.

Call
Flight call is a "weeet" or a "whititit whit."

82

Summer adult

Molting into summer plumage

Winter adult

Solitary Sandpiper
Tringa solitaria, 8½"

Main Year-round Clues
Repeatedly bobs front of body. Bold white eye-ring is complete. Back dark brown with buff to whitish spotting. Legs olive and short. Bill grayish with dark tip. Summer and winter plumages similar.

Juvenile Clues
Head and neck more evenly washed brown than streaked as in the adult.

In Flight
Dark underwings contrast with white belly. Tail dark with barring on white edges.

Call
A high-pitched "wheet wheet wheet" or "peet wheet."

Spring Migration

Seen singly or in small groups during migration, usually along edges of streams, ponds, or freshwater rivers.

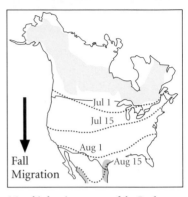

Fall Migration

Most birds migrate east of the Rocky Mountains. Migrates later than similar Spotted Sandpiper.

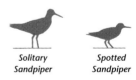

Solitary Sandpiper   **Spotted Sandpiper**

These sandpipers have similar plumage but distinctive silhouettes.

Summer adult

Winter adult

Juvenile

Wandering Tattler
Heteroscelus incanus, 11"

Main Year-round Clues
A plump, compact, gray shorebird seen on rocky coasts in winter and mountain streams in summer. Often bobs tail or front of body. Legs short, thick, yellow. Bill gray, blunt-tipped, length of head.

Additional Summer Clues
Above dark gray. Below heavily barred with gray, including undertail coverts.

Additional Winter Clues
Gray overall with a whitish belly.

In Flight
All gray above. May take zigzag flight path away from danger.

Spring Migration

In migration, found strictly on rocky coastal shores, near surf. Occurs singly or in pairs, seldom in groups of 3 or more.

Call
Repeated notes on one pitch, like "pew tu tu tu tu."

Fall Migration

Migrates over water. Does not associate with other shorebirds of rocky coasts, such as Black Turnstone, Surfbird.

Summer adult

Winter adult

In flight

Wilson's Phalarope
Phalaropus tricolor, 9¼"

Main Year-round Clues
A large-bodied, small-headed, relatively long-necked bird. Bill thin, needlelike, black, longer than length of head; bill longest of the phalaropes'. Largest phalarope; one most often seen inland. Spins around in water while feeding.

Additional Summer Clues
Female has white chin and pale gray crown; throat is cinnamon, and breast is buffy. Male has white chin and plain light brownish-gray back.

Additional Winter Clues
Back is uniformly pale gray. No dark ear patch, just pale gray line going from eye down side of neck.

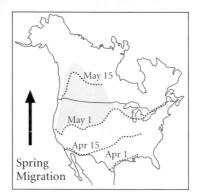

Spring Migration

Only phalarope commonly seen in central U.S. Rare on East Coast in spring; uncommon in fall.

Juvenile Clues
Like winter adult, but back has dark-centered feathers with buffy fringes. Acquires adult plumage by August.

In Flight
No wing-stripe; white rump and upper tail. Legs extend beyond tail, unlike other phalaropes'.

Fall Migration

Migrants stage in huge flocks; strong preference for saltwater lakes. Migrating females may be seen as early as June.

Call
A short grunting "ernk."

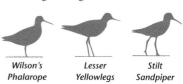

Wilson's Phalarope   Lesser Yellowlegs   Stilt Sandpiper

Similar species sometimes seen together during migration.

Summer male

Summer female

Juvenile molting into winter plumage

Red-necked Phalarope
Phalaropus lobatus, 7"

Main Year-round Clues
A compact short-necked bird. Bill thin, black, equal to depth of head; thinnest bill of phalaropes'. Smallest phalarope; usually seen along coast, but migrates north through interior West and Midwest. Spins around in water while feeding.

Additional Summer Clues
Female has white chin and dark gray crown; throat is red, and breast is gray. Male is similar but duller.

Additional Winter Clues
Dark ear patch. Back pale gray with white stripes.

Juvenile Clues
Similar face pattern to winter adult, but back is blackish, with prominent gold stripes.

In Flight
Conspicuous narrow wing-stripe. Dark central tail feathers.

Call
A low-pitched "twick."

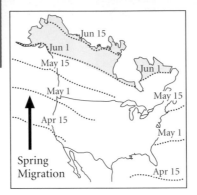

Migration mostly offshore, but also through interior West. More common and widespread than other phalaropes.

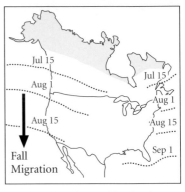

Moves south earlier, and has briefer migration period, than similar Red Phalarope; also seen nearer shore.

Red-necked Phalarope Wilson's Phalarope Red Phalarope

Bill of Red-necked is thinnest of phalaropes', about as long as head.

Adult summer male

Adult summer female

Winter adult

Juvenile

Red Phalarope
Phalaropus fulicaria, 7¾″

Main Year-round Clues

A compact short-necked bird. Bill thick, equal to or shorter than depth of head; bill is thickest of the phalaropes'. Migrates almost exclusively at sea. May spin around in water while feeding.

Additional Summer Clues

Female and male have rufous underparts and white cheeks. Bill yellow with a dark tip.

Additional Winter Clues

Dark ear patch. Back is uniformly pale gray. Bill is black (rather than yellow as in summer), sometimes with yellowish base.

Juvenile Clues

Like winter adult, but back darker and throat buffy. Use bill to distinguish from juvenile Red-necked Phalarope (p. 91).

Migration strictly oceanic, often hundreds of miles offshore. Driven to shore by storms only rarely.

In Flight

Conspicuous narrow wing-stripe. Dark central tail feathers.

Call

A shrill high-pitched "wit."

Resting migrants seen swimming and feeding on ocean surface. Typically in very large flocks. Migration period prolonged.

Red Phalarope   Wilson's Phalarope   Red-necked Phalarope

Red Phalarope's bill is thickest of phalaropes'.

Summer female

Winter

Juvenile molting into winter plumage

In flight

Ruff
Philomachus pugnax, 9–11"

Main Year-round Clues

Distinctive shape — large plump body, relatively long neck, small head. Bill relatively short, dark, slightly downcurved. Legs long, vary from orange to greenish yellow. Adult female is 2 inches smaller than male; has variable amounts of black blotches on breast; head brownish and finely streaked; tertials barred with black. Male in winter is similar but with plain gray breast; in summer, has enlarged ruff (neck) feathers that vary from black to white to reddish.

Juvenile Clues

Face, neck, upper breast buffy to grayish. Belly white. Back and wings have dark feathers with buffy edges, giving a scalloped look. Fine line trailing off behind eye. Similar to Buff-breasted Sandpiper, but 50% bigger, legs and bill longer, belly whiter.

Rare
Migrant

Rare along both Pacific and Atlantic Coasts during migration. Usually seen on grasslands or mudflats. Seen mostly Sept. to Mar. on West Coast; Apr./May and Jul./Aug. on East Coast.

In Flight

White patches on sides of rump are distinctive. Legs extend beyond tail.

Call

Usually quiet off breeding ground.

Juvenile

First decide if your bird is a plover or a sandpiper, then use the clues below to help you narrow down the choices of species. Turn to the species pages for final identification.

Killdeer is a very common shorebird of fields and mudflats. It is our only shorebird with two dark rings around its neck. P. 98.

For rare Mountain Plover, see p. 106.

Killdeer 10½″

Good Marker Bird

MEDIUM PLOVERS

♦ Short stubby bill
♦ Large eyes
♦ Feed by taking short runs, then picking food off surface

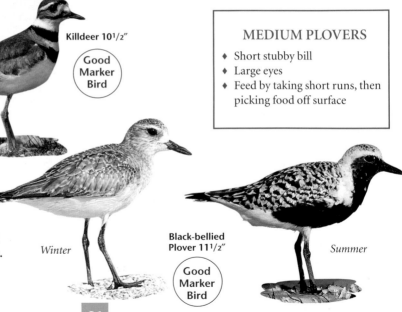

Black-bellied Plover is a very common shorebird of mudflats and seashores. It has a black belly when breeding, but in winter is white below and speckled with gray, black, and white above. P. 100. For similar but much less common golden-plovers, see pp. 102–105.

Winter

Black-bellied Plover 11½″

Good Marker Bird

Summer

MEDIUM SANDPIPERS

These sandpipers can be roughly grouped by the habitats they most frequent. Use habitat and the clues below to narrow your choices and then turn to the species description to identify your bird.

Rocky Coasts

Turnstones have short wedge-shaped bills that they often use to flip over objects while foraging. Ruddy and Black Turnstones both have dark body and white belly and appear front-heavy. Ruddy (p. 108) is particularly common.

Black Turnstone 9¹/₄″

Ruddy Turnstone 9¹/₂″

Surfbirds are heavy-looking shorebirds that feed along rocky shores in small flocks. P. 112.

Surfbird 10″

Prairies and Grasslands

Upland Sandpiper is an uncommon bird of prairies and open grassland. Its large body and small head are distinctive. P. 114.

Upland Sandpiper 12″

Buff-breasted Sandpiper is our most buffy sandpiper. Its bill is short and dark, and its legs are yellowish orange. It is an uncommon sandpiper of fields and short-grass areas. P. 116.

Buff-breasted Sandpiper 8¹/₄″

Killdeer
Charadrius vociferus, 10½″

Main Year-round Clues
Our only shorebird with two black neck-rings. Reddish-brown rump visible as bird preens. Legs pinkish gray to pale yellow. Seen in flocks on fields and mudflats during migration and in winter. Nests in fields and gravelly areas, often near human activity.

In Flight
Wide white wing-stripe; conspicuous and distinctive reddish-brown rump; long pointed tail; narrow, pointed, swept-back wings.

Call
A piercing "kihdeeah kihdeeah kihdeeah."

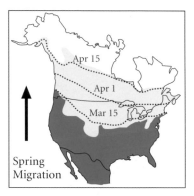

Spring Migration

Occupies wide variety of habitats. More often seen inland than at coast, especially on lawns or other short-grass areas. Often in flocks.

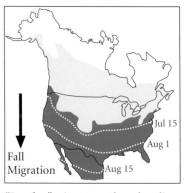

Fall Migration

"Leapfrog" migrant: northern-breeding birds go farthest south to winter, southern-breeding birds largely nonmigratory.

Long tail creates pointed shape.

Adult

Chick

Black-bellied Plover
Pluvialis squatarola, 11½"

Main Year-round Clues

Plump and rounded; short, thick, black bill; large black eye; relatively long gray to black legs; short neck. Far more common than golden-plovers. Distinctive clues in flight; see In Flight.

Additional Summer Clues

Whitish crown; chin to belly black; undertail coverts white.

Additional Winter and Juvenile Clues

Comparison with golden-plovers (GP): White belly; pale cap contrasts only slightly with white eyebrow; breast finely streaked. GPs have gray belly; dark cap contrasting strongly with white eyebrow; blurry barring or streaking on breast and belly.

Migration mostly coastal. Some first-year birds remain in winter range through summer.

In Flight

Black wingpits; bold white wing-stripe. Rump white; tail white with black bars.

Call

Plaintive 3-note whistle, like "tleeooeee."

Seen on mudflats or beaches, often in flocks of hundreds. Individual birds may use similar fall and spring routes.

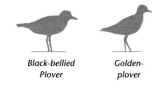

Black-bellied Plover   **Golden-plover**

Note Black-bellied Plover's shorter neck and its larger head and bill in relation to body.

Summer adult

Molting adult

Winter adult

Juvenile

In flight

American Golden-Plover
Pluvialis dominica, 10¼″

Main Year-round Clues
Plump and rounded; relatively long gray legs; short black bill; large black eye.

Additional Summer Clues
Crown dark; chin thru undertail black; undertail coverts black; flanks black; dark back feathers broadly spangled with golden edges.

Additional Winter and Juvenile Clues
Dark cap contrasts with white eyebrow; gray belly; breast and belly have subtle gray barring; back gray-brown with faint gold spots. Tips of closed wings extend well beyond tail. In primary projection, 4 to 5 primary tips extend beyond tertials. Compare with Pacific Golden-Plover (p. 104), whose overall appearance is more buff or golden buff. Juvenile has whitish eyebrow.

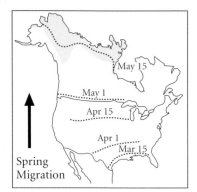

Spring Migration

Most birds use "elliptical" migration pattern: north in spring through midcontinent and south in fall over Atlantic Ocean.

Fall Migration

Most birds fly offshore, nonstop from New England to South America. Resting inland migrants usually seen in agricultural fields.

In Flight
No black wingpits or white wing-stripes. Tail, rump, and back all dark.

Call
A short "queedle."

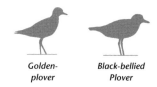

Golden-plover   Black-bellied Plover

Note golden-plover's longer neck and its smaller head and bill in relation to body.

Summer adult

Winter adult

Juvenile

Pacific Golden-Plover
Pluvialis fulva, 9¾"

Main Year-round Clues
Plump and rounded; relatively long gray legs; short, thick, black bill; large black eye.

Additional Summer Clues
Crown dark; chin to belly black; flanks and undertail coverts with some white.

Additional Winter and Juvenile Clues
Dark cap contrasts with white eyebrow; gray belly; breast and belly have subtle gray barring. Tips of closed wings extend to or just beyond tail. In primary projection, 3 primary tips extend beyond tertials. Compare with American Golden-Plover (p. 102). Juvenile has yellowish eyebrow.

In Flight
No black wingpits or white wing-stripes. Tail, rump, and back all dark.

Resting inland migrants usually seen in agricultural fields. Migration period fairly brief.

A few birds migrate along American West Coast; majority go along Asian coast or offshore to Pacific islands.

Call
Two-to-three-part whistle, "chuwi" or "chuweedle."

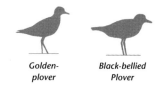

Golden-plover   Black-bellied Plover

Note golden-plover's longer neck and its smaller head and bill in relation to body.

Summer adult

Winter adult

Mountain Plover
Charadrius montanus, 9"

Main Year-round Clues
A pale long-legged plover with no neck-rings. Pale brown above; clear white below. Legs long, pale brown to pale yellow. Bill thin and all black. Usually seen on sparsely vegetated grasslands (not in mountains).

Additional Summer Clues
Forehead and lores (area between eye and base of bill) dark.

Additional Winter Clues
Forehead and lores pale.

In Flight
Pale above and white below; white patches at base of primaries seen from above.

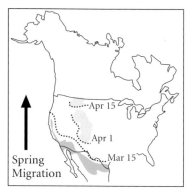

Typically migrates nonstop eastward from Pacific Coast. Not seen in mixed flocks with other shorebirds.

Widely dispersed across Great Plains in fall. Usually in flocks of 30–50 birds in short-grass prairie.

Calls
A short harsh note given during migration. Low drawn-out whistles on breeding ground.

Summer adult

Winter adult

In flight

Ruddy Turnstone
Arenaria interpres, 9½″

Main Year-round Clues
A stocky, short-legged, seemingly front-heavy shorebird. Dark bib and white belly in all plumages. Legs yellow to orange-red. Bill short, wedge-shaped, black. Forages by flipping over stones and shells with its bill, or by digging holes.

Additional Summer Clues
Back and wings bright rust-colored. Striking black-and-white markings on face of male; on female, light facial areas flecked with brown.

Additional Winter Clues
Head, back, and wings mostly brown. Black bib not as well defined and legs not as bright as in summer.

Three separate migration paths. Forms huge flocks with Red Knots and Sanderlings on Delaware Bay, fly nonstop to Hudson Bay.

In Flight
Conspicuous white stripes on back and wings. Black rump; tail white at base, black at tip.

Call
A short rattling trill.

Most often seen on bay shores or tidal flats, especially by shellfish beds. Alaska birds may go to South Pacific islands.

Summer adult

Winter adult

In flight

Black Turnstone
Arenaria melanocephala, 9¼″

Main Year-round Clues
A stocky, short-legged, seemingly front-heavy shorebird. All black except for white belly. Legs dark, tinged with red. Bill short, wedge-shaped, black. Forages by flipping over seaweed to look for food.

Additional Summer Clues
Has white spot between bill and eye.

In Flight
Conspicuous white stripes on back and wings. Black rump; tail white at base, black at tip.

Call
A short rattling trill, higher-pitched than Ruddy Turnstone's.

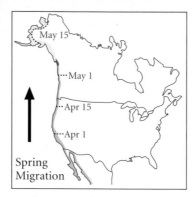

Mostly seen on rocky coastline; migrants accidental in interior West. Nonbreeders seen in winter range through summer.

Flocks with Surfbird, Rock Sandpiper, Black Oystercatcher; sometimes also with similar Ruddy Turnstone.

Summer adult

Winter adult

In flight

Surfbird
Aphriza virgata, 10"

Main Year-round Clues
A plump shorebird with a short blunt-tipped bill and short yellow legs. Feeds in rocky areas of coastline. Bill dark with yellow base of lower mandible.

Additional Summer Clues
Head and neck evenly streaked with gray. Reddish-brown patches on sides of back. Breast and sides marked with dark chevrons.

Additional Winter Clues
Dark gray above. Belly white with dark spots.

In Flight
Conspicuous white wing-stripe. Back and tail dark; rump white.

Migrants strictly coastal, but vagrants occur at Salton Sea and Central Valley of California.

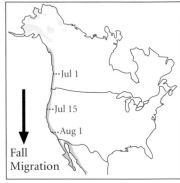

Nearly always seen on rocky shores, jetties. Gregarious; in flocks of hundreds, often with turnstones or Rock Sandpipers.

Call
Winter flocks give soft high-pitched whistles.

Summer adult

Winter adult

In flight

Upland Sandpiper
Bartramia longicauda, 12"

Main Year-round Clues

Usually seen in grasslands. A large-bodied shorebird with a small head, short bill, and long neck. Legs long and yellow. Bill short and mostly yellow, with darker tip. Long tail projects well past wing tips. Same plumage all year.

In Flight

All brown above with darker rump and wing tips; underwings strongly barred with black and white. Long tail. Flies with stiff bowed wings in display over breeding grounds. May hold wings up briefly after landing.

Call

On breeding ground gives a loud "wolf whistle," like "wheet wheeuuu." Flight call a loud rolling "do do do du."

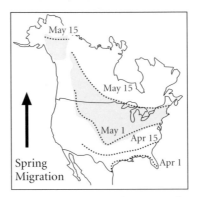

Seldom seen near water; favors mowed or unmowed grasslands. Seen mostly alone or in pairs.

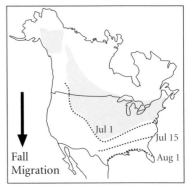

Rare on West Coast, uncommon on East Coast. Most birds gather on western Gulf Coast and fly nonstop to South America.

Adult

Adult

Main Year-round Clues

Distinctive clear buffy face, breast, and belly. Bill short, dark. Legs yellow. Generally seen in fields or short-grass areas. Summer and winter plumages similar.

In Flight

Wings have bright white undersides with dark "comma" at wrist; dark rump; no wing-stripe.

Call

Flight call is a low "pr-r-reet." Usually silent off breeding ground.

Migration period very brief; shorter than that of other shorebirds. Few seen outside narrow midcontinental migration path.

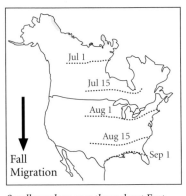

Small numbers seen throughout East. Favors dry areas like fields, where found with golden-plovers, Baird's Sandpipers.

Summer adult

Juvenile

Clues to Small Shorebirds

6–8" Size of Sparrow

First use the boxed tips to help you decide if your small shorebird is a plover or a sandpiper, then use the clues and photos to help you narrow down the choices of species. Turn to the species pages for final identification.

Snowy Plover is the smallest and has a relatively thin pointed bill for a plover. P. 124

Snowy Plover 6¹⁄₄″

Wilson's Plover is the largest and has a noticeably larger bill than the other small plovers. P. 126.

Wilson's Plover 7³⁄₄″

SMALL PLOVERS

♦ Short stubby bill
♦ Large eyes
♦ Feed by taking short runs, then picking food off surface
♦ Neck ring

Semipalmated and Piping Plovers are similar. Both have short stubby bills that are orange at the base in summer and usually all black in winter. Both have orange to yellowish legs.

The Semipalmated Plover is dark-backed, has a wide complete neck-ring, and is abundant. P. 120.

Semipalmated Plover 7¹⁄₄″

Good Marker Bird

The Piping Plover is pale-backed, has a thin neck-ring, and is uncommon. P. 122.

Piping Plover 7¹⁄₄″

Least Sandpiper is the smallest and has yellowish legs. P. 128.

Least Sandpiper 6"

Good Marker Bird

Western Sandpiper has a longer slightly downturned bill and is present in N. Am. in winter. P. 130.

Western Sandpiper 6½"

These two are just slightly larger than Least Sandpiper.

Semipalmated Sandpiper has a straight tubular bill; usually not present in N. Am. in winter. P. 132.

Semipalmated Sandpiper 6¼"

SMALL SANDPIPERS

♦ Thin pointed bill
♦ Smaller eyes
♦ Feed by walking and repeatedly probing for food

White-rumped Sandpiper has a white rump (seen in flight) and streaking along flanks. P. 134.

White-rumped Sandpiper 7½"

These two are substantially larger than the Least Sandpiper.

Baird's Sandpiper has a dark rump and clear white flanks. P. 136.

Baird's Sandpiper 7½"

"Wave Chaser"
The small sandpiper that continually chases the edges of ocean waves as it feeds. P. 138

Sanderling 8"

Good Marker Bird

"Bobber"
Continually bobs tail as it walks; has no spots in winter. P. 140. Found along lakes and rivers.

Spotted Sandpiper 7½"

Semipalmated Plover
Charadrius semipalmatus, 7¼″

Main Year-round Clues
A small, plump, dark-backed plover. Bill stubby, all black or black with orange base. Neck-ring wide, complete, black. Legs dull yellow to orange.

Additional Summer Clues
Forehead, eye-stripe, and neck-ring black in male, dark brown in female. Bill black with orange base.

Additional Winter Clues
Forehead, eye-stripe, and neck-ring brown in both sexes. Bill all black; may have some orange at base.

In Flight
Thin white wing-stripe; dark tail with white edges.

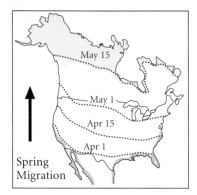

Spring Migration

Most birds migrate along the coast; seen in smaller numbers inland. Commonly occurs in mixed flocks.

Fall Migration

Most numerous on East Coast. Migration is prolonged, lasting into November.

Call
A short note followed by rising whistle, like "ch'wheeet." A churring sound when defending a feeding area.

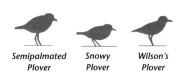

Semipalmated Plover   **Snowy Plover**   **Wilson's Plover**

Note differences in bill shapes and sizes.

Summer adult female

Summer adult male

Winter adult

Piping Plover
Charadrius melodus, 7¼″

Main Year-round Clues
A small, pale-backed, stubby-billed plover. Bill short and thick, all black or black with orange base. Neck-ring thin, sometimes incomplete. Legs bright yellow to orange.

Additional Summer Clues
Neck-ring thin and black in male, dark brown in female. Bill black with orange base.

Additional Winter Clues
Bill usually all black. Neck-ring thin and grayish.

In Flight
Narrow wing-stripe; white rump; white edges to dark tail.

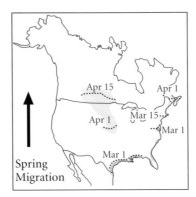

Inland migrants gather on Gulf Coast, then migrate nonstop to Midwest. East Coast migrants move north earlier.

Occasionally seen inland in Atlantic Coast states. Rarely seen in flocks of more than 6 birds.

Call
A whistled "peeep" or two-note "peep-low."

| Piping Plover | Snowy Plover | Wilson's Plover |

Note differences in bill shapes and sizes.

Summer adult male

Summer adult female

Winter adult

Snowy Plover
Charadrius alexandrinus, 6¼"

Main Year-round Clues
Small, pale-backed, and relatively long-legged plover. Bill black, thin, and pointed. Legs dark gray to black. Neck-ring incomplete. Gulf Coast race is color of pale sand on back; western race is slightly darker.

Additional Summer Clues
Male has forehead, ear patch, and partial neck-ring all black. Female has these areas all brown.

Additional Winter Clues
Both sexes look similar to summer female.

In Flight
Narrow wing-stripe; wide white borders to dark rump.

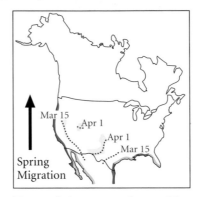

Two populations: one goes between West Coast and Salt Lake area, the other between Gulf Coast and south-central U.S.

Many birds are year-round residents along both Gulf Coast and West Coast.

Call
Whistled "ku-wheet."

Snowy Plover   Semipalmated Plover   Wilson's Plover

Note differences in bill shapes and sizes.

Summer adult male

Summer adult female

Flock in flight

Wilson's Plover
Charadrius wilsonia, 7¾"

Main Year-round Clues
A small, dark-backed, large-billed plover. Bill noticeably large, long, and black; the "Jimmy Durante" of small plovers. Neck-ring complete and broad; black in male; brown in female. Legs dull pinkish to gray. Long wings and long bill give it an attenuated look; usually runs or skulks along in horizontal posture. The largest "small ring-necked plover." Often on mudflats.

In Flight
Thin white wing-stripe and dark tail.

Call
A short, sharp, rising whistle, like someone calling a dog — "wheet" or "wheet wheet."

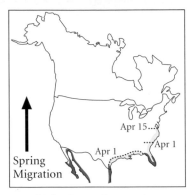

Some birds migrate along Mexican coast to Gulf states. Florida wintering birds go up East Coast.

Two separate migration routes as in spring. Migrants occur in small groups on coastal beaches.

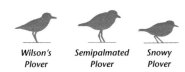

Note differences in bill shapes and sizes.

Summer adult male

Winter adult

Least Sandpiper
Calidris minutilla, 6"

Main Year-round Clues
Our smallest sandpiper; generally appears dark brown and small-headed. Legs yellowish; all other small sandpipers have blackish legs. Bill black, short, finely pointed, drooping slightly at the tip. Often feeds farther up from shoreline than other sandpipers and appears hunched over as it feeds.

Additional Summer Clues
Dark brown breast and very dark back.

Additional Winter Clues
Back and wing feathers have dark brown centers and lighter edges, creating a "scaled" appearance; breast streaked with light brown.

Juvenile Clues
Sharply patterned rufous-and-black back.

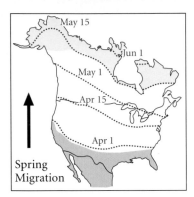

Spring Migration

Eastern birds appear to be "elliptical migrants": use interior route in spring, East Coast route in fall.

In Flight
Appears darker and smaller than other "peeps." Narrow white wing-stripe; dark central tail.

Call
Like its name (Least), its call has a strong "eee" sound, like "kreeet."

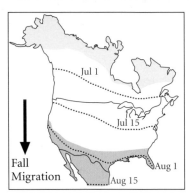

Fall Migration

Frequents areas that are grassier than those visited by other small sandpipers. Gregarious; occasionally occurs in flocks of thousands.

Least Sandpiper   Western Sandpiper   Dunlin

All three species have slightly down-curved bills. Note size differences and relative bill lengths.

Summer adult

Worn summer adult

Winter adult

Juvenile

Western Sandpiper
Calidris mauri, 6½"

Main Year-round Clues
Legs black. Bill black, relatively long, broad at base, tapers to fine point, droops slightly at tip. Grayish-brown appearance.

Additional Summer Clues
Rufous crown and ear patch. Rufous bases to scapular feathers. Dark chevrons along flanks.

Additional Winter Clues
Gray above. Longer-billed, more uniformly colored grayish back, and whiter-breasted than Least Sandpiper (p. 128); smaller, darker-faced than Sanderling (p. 138) and with no dark shoulder.

Juvenile Clues
Wide rufous edges of upper scapulars contrast with gray wings and back.

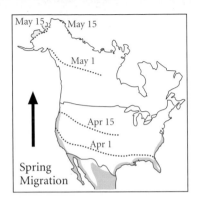

Most birds move along Pacific Coast; few in interior. Some nonbreeding birds stay on eastern Gulf Coast all summer.

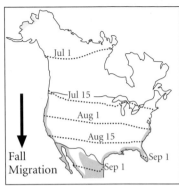

More widespread than in spring; common in central states. Unlike other small sandpipers, migrates in a series of short flights.

In Flight
Narrow white wing-stripe. Dark central tail feathers.

Call
A buzzy "dzheeet."

Western   Semipalmated
Sandpiper   Sandpiper

Very similar species. Note bill shape and length.

Summer adult

Adult molting to summer plumage

Winter adult

Juvenile

Semipalmated Sandpiper
Calidris pusilla, 6¼"

Main Year-round Clues
Legs black (can be tinged with gray). Bill black, short, tubular, blunt-tipped, straight with little or no droop, thick at base. Grayish-brown appearance. Does not winter in U.S. Bills finer-tipped and longer (on average) in East, blunter and shorter in West.

Additional Summer Clues
Grayish brown above with little or no rufous on back or head. Black-centered scapulars contrast strongly with other back feathers. Flanks have few or no spots. Eastern birds can appear much more rufous overall in spring.

Juvenile Clues (seen July–Oct.)
Buffy to grayish brown, with little or no rufous on back or head. When rufous is present on back feathers, it is confined to fringes. More uniform scaly appearance to upperparts than Western Sandpiper.

Majority pass through central states. Multitudes stage at Delaware Bay and at Cheyenne Bottoms in Kansas.

In Flight
Thin wing-stripe; dark central tail feathers.

Call
A short "cherk."

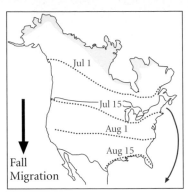

Unlike in spring, common on Northeast Coast; many birds fly nonstop from New England to South America.

| Semipalmated Sandpiper | Western Sandpiper |

Very similar species. Note bill shape and length.

132

Summer adults (eastern birds)

Molting adult

Winter adult

Juvenile

White-rumped Sandpiper
Calidris fuscicollis, 7½"

Main Year-round Clues
Long wings and short legs create a more attenuated and horizontal posture than that of smaller sandpipers. Generally grayer than Baird's Sandpiper (p. 136). White rump seen during preening and in flight. Legs black. Bill black, slightly downcurved; thicker based and more curved than Baird's. Wing tips extend well beyond tail (also true of Baird's); wing tips of other small sandpipers do not extend past tip of tail. Winter plumage rarely seen in U.S.

Additional Summer Clues
Dark streaks on breast extend well along flanks toward tail. Reddish on back and crown. Base of lower bill orangish.

Juvenile Clues
White lines on back. Bold white eyebrow. No streaking on flanks.

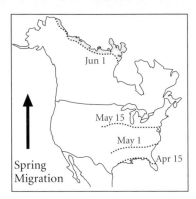

"Long-hop" migration: birds gather in central states, then fly nonstop overland to breeding grounds.

Most do not pass through U.S. but fly directly from eastern Canada nonstop over the Atlantic to South America.

In Flight
Distinctive white rump clearly visible. Narrow white wing-stripe.

Call
High-pitched "jeeet."

White-rumped Sandpiper   **Western Sandpiper**   **Least Sandpiper**

All three species have slightly down-curved bills. Subtle differences in body shape and proportions are useful identifiers.

Summer adult

Winter adult

Juvenile

In flight

Baird's Sandpiper
Calidris bairdii, 7½"

Main Year-round Clues

Long wings and short legs create a more attenuated and horizontal posture than that of smaller sandpipers. Generally buffier than White-rumped Sandpiper (p. 134) — "Baird's is buffy." Legs black. Bill slender and black, slightly shorter and straighter than White-rumped's. Wing tips extend well beyond tail (also true of White-rumped); wing tips of other small sandpipers do not extend past tip of tail. Winter plumage rarely seen in U.S.

Additional Summer Clues

Fine buffy-brown streaks on breast. No streaking along flanks. Dark rump.

Juvenile Clues

No white lines on back. Upperparts pale gray and scaly, with no red on scapulars.

Spring Migration

Found in areas that are drier than those visited by other small sandpipers. Occurs in fields with Pectoral and Buff-breasted Sandpipers, golden-plovers.

Eyebrow faint; not bold and white as in White-rumped juvenile. Flanks unstreaked.

In Flight

Narrow white wing-stripe. Dark rump.

Fall Migration

More widespread than in spring. Uncommon east of Mississippi River, where birds seen are mostly late-migrating juveniles.

Call

Low trilling "preet" or a guttural "krrrt."

Baird's Sandpiper   Semipalmated Sandpiper

Note head-to-body proportions.

Summer adult

Juvenile

Sanderling
Calidris alba, 8"

Main Year-round Clues
Most common small shorebird chasing waves in and out along the shore. Black legs seem a blur as it runs. Bill short, tubular, black. Larger and chunkier than other small sandpipers. Usually in flocks.

Additional Summer Clues
Head, breast, and back orange-brown with brown streaking. Belly white.

Additional Winter Clues
Face whiter than on other small sandpipers. Crown and back gray; belly white. Patch of black feathers on shoulder. Juvenile birds have some black feathers on back.

In Flight
Pale back with conspicuous white wing-stripes.

Spring Migration

Most numerous in East, where seen in extraordinary numbers at Delaware Bay with knots and turnstones.

Fall Migration

Unlike other small sandpipers, most commonly seen at beaches, feeding in path of receding waves.

Call
A "kip" in flight.

Sanderling   **Western Sandpiper**   **Semipalmated Sandpiper**

Note differences in sizes and body proportions.

Summer adult

Molting into winter plumage

Winter adult

Juvenile

Spotted Sandpiper
Actitis macularia, 7½″

Main Year-round Clues
Continually bobs tail while walking. A notch of white in front of folded wing. Legs usually yellowish. Frequents lake and stream edges. See In Flight.

Additional Summer Clues
Upperparts brown with a few black bars. Underparts white with large dark spots. Bill orange with a darker tip.

Additional Winter Clues
Upperparts brown; underparts pure white. Bill dark with some orange at base.

In Flight
Distinctive flight — bird flies close to water with shallow, stiff wingbeats. Conspicuous wing-stripe.

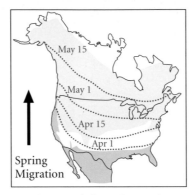

Found in many habitats, but nearly always along watery shores. Most numerous in interior states.

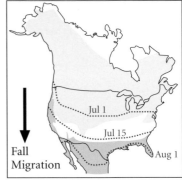

Seen alone or in small groups. In fall, more numerous in coastal states than in interior.

Call
Loud, repeated, upslurred whistles, like "weet weet weet" or "peet weet."

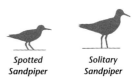

Spotted Sandpiper   **Solitary Sandpiper**

These sandpipers have similar plumage but distinctive silhouettes.

Summer adult

Winter adult

Juvenile

Adult in flight

Rare Sandpipers

There are many other shorebirds that only rarely show up in North America. Here are four of the most commonly occurring rarities in the plumages in which they are most likely to be seen. In North America, these birds are almost exclusively seen on the coasts.

Red-necked Stint
Calidris ruficollis, 6"

Breeding adult is plumage most often seen. Brick-red on head, neck, throat, and upper breast. Dark streaks at base of red on upper breast. Reddish color can fade on chin and throat by early fall. Bill short and blunt-tipped. Wing coverts plain gray.

Little Stint
Calidris minuta, 6"

Breeding adult is plumage most often seen. Very similar to the Red-necked Stint. Face and sides of breast rufous. Chin, neck, and central breast white. Bill short and slightly finer tipped than Red-necked Stint. Wing coverts edged with rufous. Long thin legs.

Red-necked Stint, summer adult

Little Stint, summer adult

Sharp-tailed Sandpiper
Calidris acuminata, 8½"

Curlew Sandpiper
Calidris ferruginea, 8½"

Juvenal plumage is most often seen. Size and shape of Pectoral Sandpiper (p. 78). Bright orange-buff wash mostly on sides; relatively unstreaked breast. Bright rufous crown. Bold white eyebrow.

Breeding plumage most often seen. Long evenly downcurved bill. Deep chestnut on head, breast, and belly. Mottled chestnut back. Birds in transition to winter show patches of gray in chestnut areas.

Sharp-tailed Sandpiper, juvenile

Curlew Sandpiper, summer adult (left)

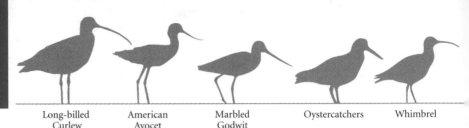

Silhouettes of North American Shorebirds

Arranged from Largest to Smallest

Long-billed Curlew | American Avocet | Marbled Godwit | Oystercatchers | Whimbrel

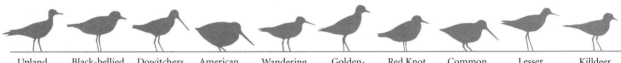

Upland Sandpiper | Black-bellied Plover | Dowitchers | American Woodcock | Wandering Tattler | Golden-Plovers | Red Knot | Common Snipe | Lesser Yellowlegs | Killdeer

Pectoral Sandpiper | Red Phalarope | Dunlin | Stilt Sandpiper | Solitary Sandpiper | Buff-breasted Sandpiper | Sanderling | Red-necked Phalarope | Wilson's Plover | Baird's Sandpiper | White-rumped Sandpiper

144